Alexander
the Great

These and other titles are included in The Importance
Of biography series:

Alexander the Great
Napoleon Bonaparte
Cleopatra
Christopher Columbus
Marie Curie
Thomas Edison
Albert Einstein
Benjamin Franklin
Galileo Galilei
Jim Henson
Thomas Jefferson
Chief Joseph
Malcolm X

Margaret Mead
Michelangelo
Wolfgang Amadeus Mozart
Sir Isaac Newton
Richard M. Nixon
Jackie Robinson
Anwar Sadat
Margaret Sanger
John Steinbeck
Jim Thorpe
Mark Twain
H.G. Wells

Alexander the Great

by
Gail B. Stewart

Lucent Books, P.O. Box 289011, San Diego, CA 92198-9011

Library of Congress Cataloging-in-Publication Data

Stewart, Gail, 1949-
   Alexander the Great / by Gail B. Stewart
      p. cm.—(Importance of)
   Includes bibliographical references and index.
   ISBN 1-56006-047-6
   1. Alexander, the Great, 356-323 B.C.—Juvenile literature.
2. Greece—Kings and rulers—Biography—Juvenile literature.
3. Generals—Greece—Biography—Juvenile literature. 4.
Greece—History—Macedonian Expansion, 359-323 B.C.—Juvenile literature. [1. Alexander, the Great, 356-323 B.C. 2. Kings,
queens, rulers, etc. 3. Generals. 4. Greece—History—Macedonian Expansion, 359-323 B.C.] I.Title. II. Title: Importance of
Alexander the Great. III. Series.
DF234.S74   1994
938.07'092—dc20   93-39983
[B]   CIP
                                                                 AC

Contents

Foreword

THE IMPORTANCE OF biography series deals with individuals who have made a unique contribution to history. The editors of the series have deliberately chosen to cast a wide net and include people from all fields of endeavor. Individuals from politics, music, art, literature, philosophy, science, sports, and religion are all represented. In addition, the editors did not restrict the series to individuals whose accomplishments have helped change the course of history. Of necessity, this criterion would have eliminated many whose contribution was great, though limited. Charles Darwin, for example, was responsible for radically altering the scientific view of the natural history of the world. His achievements continue to impact the study of science today. Others, such as Chief Joseph of the Nez Percé, played a pivotal role in the history of their own people. While Joseph's influence does not extend much beyond the Nez Percé, his nonviolent resistance to white expansion and his continuing role in protecting his tribe and his homeland remain an inspiration to all.

These biographies are more than factual chronicles. Each volume attempts to emphasize an individual's contributions both in his or her own time and for posterity. For example, the voyages of Christopher Columbus opened the way to European colonization of the New World. Unquestionably, his encounter with the New World brought monumental changes to both Europe and the Americas in his day. Today, however, the broader impact of Columbus's voyages is being critically scrutinized. *Christopher Columbus,* as well as every biography in The Importance Of series, includes and evaluates the most recent scholarship available on each subject.

Each author includes a wide variety of primary and secondary source quotations to document and substantiate his or her work. All quotes are footnoted to show readers exactly how and where biographers derive their information, as well as provide stepping stones to further research. These quotations enliven the text by giving readers eyewitness views of the life and times of each individual covered in The Importance Of series.

Finally, each volume is enhanced by photographs, bibliographies, chronologies, and comprehensive indexes. For both the casual reader and the student engaged in research, The Importance Of biographies will be a fascinating adventure into the lives of people who have helped shape humanity's past, present, and will continue to shape its future.

Important Dates in the Life of Alexander the Great

B.C.

Philip becomes king of Macedon. — **359**

357 — Philip marries Olympias of Epirus.

Alexander born in Pella, capital of — **356**
Macedon.

344 — Alexander impresses his father by subduing the wild horse Bucephalas.

Alexander studies under the Greek — **343-**
philosopher Aristotle. **340**

Philip goes to war against the Greek city-state and lets Alexander head the cavalry in the battle of Chaeronea.

Philip marries a Macedonian woman; **338**
Alexander and his father quarrel at the
wedding.

337 — Philip is assassinated by one of his bodyguards; the army hails Alexander as the new king of Macedon.

Alexander leads his army into battle — **336**
against the northern provinces; defeats
the city of Thebes.

335 — Alexander crosses the Hellespont and begins his campaign against Darius's Persian Empire; fights his first battle against the Great King at the Granicus River.

Visits Gordium and cuts the famous — **334**
knot; defeats the Persians at the battle
of Issus in the fall. **333**

Alexander's forces defeat Darius at the **332**
battle of Gaugamela; Alexander occupies the Persian cities of Susa, Babylon,
and Persepolis. **331**

For seven months Alexander's army works to topple the city of Tyre; after the fall of Tyre, Alexander goes on to Egypt.

Alexander crosses the Hindu Kush **330**
mountains; Bessus is captured and executed for the murder of Darius. **329**

Darius killed by Bessus; Philotas and Parmenio killed.

Alexander kills Cleitus.

The Macedonians defeat Porus at the **328**
Hydaspes River; threatened mutiny of
Alexander's army; Alexander's horse **327**
Bucephalus dies; Alexander gravely
wounded in the battle with the Malli. **326**

Alexander begins his invasion of India; marries Roxane after the battle against Oxyartes at Sogdiana.

Alexander splits his troops and tries to — **325**
march parallel to his sailors; experiences heavy troop losses in difficult
march through the desert. **324**

Alexander holds huge wedding ceremony and arranges the marriage of ninety of his officers; takes thirty thousand young Persian soldiers into his army; Alexander's troops become angry with him for his apparent favoritism of Persians; his beloved friend Hephestion dies.

Alexander dies in Babylon. **323**

King, Master, Pharaoh, God

He was only thirty-three years old when he died—young even by the standards of the third century B.C. He had fought the stabbing stomach cramps and high fever for eleven days, and some of his advisors believed he might rally. Friends visited temples and shrines throughout Babylon, praying to various gods to spare their leader's life.

But in the end it was clear that death was very near. The side doors to his bedchamber were opened and his men—soldiers who had fought bravely for him—were allowed to file through to say goodbye. Although Alexander was gravely ill, he still managed to summon the energy to respond to each of his men. As the ancient historian Arrian writes, not a single man went through the line without being acknowledged. "They say he was speechless as the army filed past. Yet he greeted one and all, raising his head, though with difficulty, and signing to them with his eyes."[1]

When death came at last, Alexander's advisors decided that their leader should be honored in a spectacular funeral, unlike anything the world had ever seen. After all, this was no mere king or emperor—Alexander had conquered the world. At the time of his death, he was the emperor of Greece, the king of Persia, the supreme ruler of Asia (including India), and the grand pharaoh of Egypt. Alexander was a man without equal in history; many in his empire half-believed that he was more god than mortal. It seemed only fitting that his funeral should be more magnificent than anything real or imagined.

Alexander the Great, whose military genius was unequaled in the ancient world.

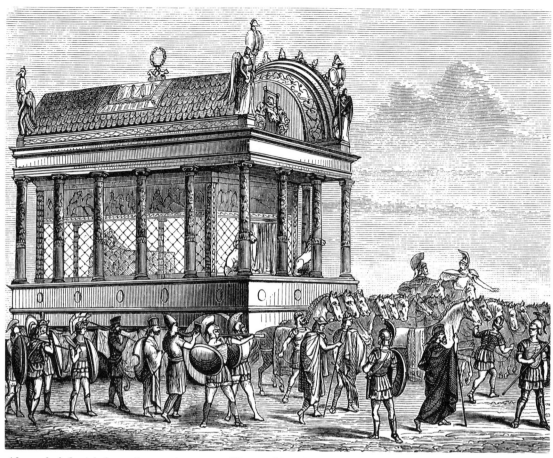

Alexander's lavish funeral procession was unlike anything the ancient world had seen. Spectators came from afar to behold the golden, bejeweled temple.

A Temple on Wheels

Although Alexander had died in Babylon, his advisors made plans for his body to be taken to Macedon for burial. Macedon, north of Greece, had been Alexander's home, the land from which he began his conquests, and it was customary in those times for a king to be buried in the place of his beginnings.

The body was embalmed with sweet-smelling spices and incense, while the most skilled craftspeople began building the funeral car. The task took more than two years. When the car was completed, it led the funeral procession on its long journey which began in Babylon. One ancient historian, Diodorus of Sicily, provides a detailed description of the procession, although "it appeared more magnificent when seen than when described."[2]

The car carrying the royal coffin (which was made of solid gold) was a golden temple on wheels. The temple had sixteen golden columns which supported a roof made of layered gold embedded with hundreds of precious jewels. On each of the temple's four sides were colorful paintings depicting Alexander's most famous battles. The four wheels supporting the car were decorated with golden lions, each holding a spear in its teeth. A spun-gold net hung from the roof of the temple, filling the spaces between the columns and screening the coffin from the wind and rain, but not from the eyes of the curious crowds who came to catch a glimpse of the royal funeral.

And what a spectacle the crowds saw! First came the road builders, scurrying before the funeral car, smoothing the path to keep it from bumping. Sixty-four mules set in teams of four, pulled the car. Golden bells hung from their cheeks and harnesses, which were lavishly speckled with rubies and diamonds. Following last were the thousands of men who had been Alexander's loyal soldiers, riding in silence behind their king. It was a slow, careful march; on most days the funeral moved no more than eight or ten miles. An endless stream of people came to see the procession, chanting prayers and singing songs of praise to the great Alexander.

"Because of [the funeral's] widespread fame, it drew together many spectators," writes Diodorus, "for from every city into which it came the whole people went forth to meet it and again escorted it on its way out, not becoming sated with the pleasure of beholding it."[3]

The Prestige of a Tomb

When the procession reached Syria, it was rerouted. Ptolemy, one of Alexander's generals, had been left in charge of Egypt after Alexander's armies had conquered it. He met the procession and suggested an alternate burial site. Why take Alexander's body back to Macedon, when in life the Great King had never shown any interest in returning home? Instead, Ptolemy insisted that the funeral procession continue west, toward Egypt, and that he should lead it there. Alexander would be laid to rest in the city he had founded himself: Alexandria, on the coast of the Mediterranean Sea.

So the funeral edged on, the golden bells of the mules ringing across the hot desert sands to Egypt until they reached the dead king's city, Alexandria. Ptolemy, according to historians, had other reasons for bringing Alexander's body back to Egypt. He wanted to retain control of Egypt and was worried that rivals were beginning a military campaign to unseat him as governor. Ptolemy needed the support of a strong army, and he felt that bringing Alexander's body to Egypt for entombment would increase his own status.

As it later turned out, Ptolemy made the right decision. He became famous and was admired for bringing Alexander's body back to Egypt. According to Diodorus:

> Because of [Ptolemy's] graciousness and nobility of heart, men came together eagerly from all sides to Alexandria and gladly enrolled for the campaign, although the army of the [rival] kings was about to fight against that of Ptolemy; and, even though the risks were manifest and great, yet all of them willingly took upon themselves at their personal risk the preservation of Ptolemy's safety.[4]

Even though the man was dead, Alexander's power was astonishing.

A miniature from a fifteenth-century manuscript shows Alexander in battle with monstrous creatures. Even today, the legend of Alexander continues to captivate artists and writers.

What Sort of Man?

Thirty-three when he died and barely twenty when he began his career—it seems unbelievable that a person could have accomplished so much in thirteen years. Yet these accomplishments remain controversial. Some historians praise Alexander as the first global thinker, one who united the cultures and peoples his armies subdued. Others, like historian Jacob Abbott, are less glowing in their appraisals of Alexander. "He was simply a robber," writes Abbott, "but yet a robber on so vast a scale, that mankind, in contemplating his career, [has] generally lost sight of the wickedness of his crimes in their admiration of the enormous magnitude of the scale on which they were perpetrated."[5]

A world conqueror, a robber, a master strategist, a military genius, a leader of men—what sort of man was Alexander the Great? And how is the world different because of his accomplishments?

Chapter

1 The Roots of an Earthshaker

Alexander grew up in a kingdom north of Greece, called Macedon. Today no such country exists; what once was Macedon is spread over the modern-day nations of Bulgaria, Russia, and what was, until recently, the nation of Yugoslavia. In Alexander's day, however, Macedon was a thriving, important place, ruled by one of the most powerful men in the ancient world. The man was known as Philip of Macedon, and it is impossible to imagine any other man as Alexander the Great's father.

Most kings and emperors in history inherited their titles. Passing down the crown from parent to child is the nature of royalty. But never in history has a ruler acquired as much from his royal father as Alexander. In fact, historian C.L. Sulzberger dubs Philip and Alexander "the outstanding father-son team of temporal leadership so far produced by mankind."[6] One cannot begin to understand the magnificent achievements of Alexander's short life without understanding the influence and accomplishments of his father Philip.

A Land of Barbarians

Macedon's power and influence in the fourth century B.C. was due almost entirely to Philip. Before Philip's rule, the Greeks held the most power and influence. Greece in this long-ago time was not a single nation, but rather a collection of individual states, each with its own government.

The Greeks did not derive their power from military might, although Greece had its share of war heroes. Instead, the ancient Greeks placed higher regard on thought and the cultivation of new ideas than on increasing the size of the Greek

Source: The World Book Encyclopedia.

The ancient Greek city-state of Sparta as it may have looked in the fourth century B.C.

realm. Great achievements in architecture, art, and philosophical thought separated the Greeks from others in the ancient world. The Greeks invented the system of democracy in government and were the first to begin a scientific method of catego-

rizing living things. They excelled in drama and literature and were the first to speculate on the nature of atoms.

Although Macedon's people spoke the same language as the Greeks, they were not Greek in the same way as their neigh-

Art, sculpture, and philosophical thought flourished in ancient Greece. These Greek vases show the artistry of the ancient Athenians.

bor to the south—the Greeks of Athens, Sparta, Thebes, and other important city-states. They were not philosophers, sculptors, or mathematicians. Instead, as historian Nicholas Hammond reports, they were

> physically tough through the open-air life in a country of harsh winters and torrid summers, sturdily independent in the face of constant dangers, hard working and hard fighting. . . . They had not had the time or the means to engage in soft and luxurious living, as some of their neighbors to the south.[7]

They were farmers and herders, and their culture was tribal, centered more on smaller rural living groups than on city governments. Because of this, the Greeks tended to think of the Macedonians as non-Greek, and referred to them as *barbaroi*, or "barbarians." Even though the Macedonian royalty claimed that they were descendants of the legendary Greek hero Hercules, who was himself thought to be the son of a god, the Macedonians were definitely second-rate in Greek eyes.

From Hostage to King

Philip was the son of the Macedonian king Amyntas II. During Philip's childhood, a great deal of political unrest existed between Macedon and the Greek state of Thebes. As part of a diplomatic bargain, the Thebans had asked that the young prince, who was then sixteen years old, be brought to Thebes as a sort of hostage until the problems could be worked out.

For four years Philip lived away from home among the Theban people. Philip gained a great deal from his stay in Thebes. He was not only educated at fine Greek schools, but also received military training from the Theban general Epaminondas, the most renowned soldier in Greece. From Epaminondas Philip learned the art

Theban general Epaminondas displayed great military skill and courage in battle. Under Epaminondas's tutelage, Philip became a strong and seasoned warrior.

of soldiering, knowledge that was to serve him well in the years ahead.

Testing King Philip

After Philip was allowed to return to Macedon in 359 B.C., his elder brother, who had become king after the death of their father, was killed in battle. At the age of twenty, Philip inherited the throne. The task of governing Macedon belonged to him, and it was not going to be easy.

From every direction, it seemed, there were challenges for the new king. Philip had to face rivals within his own kingdom—people who felt they were better

Philip became king of Macedon at the age of twenty. A shrewd and capable leader, he paved the way for Alexander's later triumphs.

equipped to handle the responsibility of king. Outside the country's borders, rival tribes hoping to increase their territory were anxious to invade Macedon. With its new, inexperienced king, the country seemed an easy target.

But Philip was not intimidated by any of these rivals. The years spent in Thebes had taught him to act quickly and decisively against his enemies. As historian John Snyder writes:

> In swift succession, rival claims to the [throne] were brushed aside; their holders were killed or exiled. The barbarian Illyrian tribes to the northwest were tamed with similar speed. Combining dissimulation [cunning] with bribery, trickery, and lightning attack when necessary, the new [king] reduced them to the status of vassals.[8]

Once his title as king was no longer disputed, Philip began forging an aggressive, well-trained army that could not only defend Macedon, but could also expand the nation's borders. In this endeavor, King Philip was remarkably successful. "Security snowballed into new opportunism," writes one historian. "Each gain brought more men and revenues, more rich pastures on which more cavalrymen could be maintained for yet more conquest."[9]

This was the beginning of a new Macedon, a nation that was earning the respect of all its neighbors, including the Greeks. In the years of Philip's reign, Macedon would become the mightiest force in that part of the world. Historians agree that it was Philip who laid the strong foundation for his famous son's later conquests.

"The Macedon that Alexander inherited," writes historian A.B. Bosworth, "was the creation of his father. The army he led was forged by Philip. The material resources of the Macedonian throne were acquired by Philip. . . . In his first years, at least, Alexander was continuing a process begun by his father."[10]

Prayers and Snakes by the Light of the Moon

But Philip was not the only early influence in Alexander's life. While Alexander acquired his ambition and his knowledge of soldiering from his father, in temperament he was remarkably similar to his mother, Queen Olympias.

Olympias was the daughter of the king of Epirus, a mountainous region southwest of Macedon, in what is today called Albania. As Philip began expanding the borders of his kingdom, he turned to Epirus. He struck a deal with Epirus's king; if he

married the king's daughter, he would be free to swallow up the territory of Epirus, without any struggle. Such an arrangement was a marriage of convenience, a common occurrence in those times.

If Philip had planned on a docile, submissive wife from the bargain, he was greatly mistaken. Olympias was ambitious, emotional, and fiercely independent. She was very proud of the fact that her family descended directly from the Greek legendary warrior, Achilles, a hero of the Trojan War.

Olympias was also a member of a secret religious cult which practiced wild nighttime dances under the moon. Like other members of her cult, Olympias drank wine and claimed to have prophetic visions during these ceremonies. And if ancient historians such as Plutarch can be believed, Olympias was even more passionate than others in her fervent dances and prayers to the gods:

It was Olympias's habit to enter into these [rituals] and surrender herself to the inspiration of the god with even wilder abandon than the others, and she would introduce into the . . . procession numbers of large snakes, hand-tamed, which terrified the male spectators as they raised their heads from the wreaths of ivy and the sacred winnowing baskets, or twined themselves around the wands and garlands of the women.[11]

The wild, impetuous Olympias became the new queen of Macedon in 357 B.C. by marrying King Philip, a rising star in the ancient Greek world. The child born of that marriage was Alexander.

Omens and Signs

Like many people of the time, Olympias and Philip believed in omens and signs and had faith that much could be predicted by dreams. Olympias's dream on her wedding night was therefore important to her. According to Plutarch, she dreamed that her womb was suddenly struck by a thunderbolt, an event that was followed by a blinding flash "from which a great sheet of flame blazed up and spread far and wide before it finally died away."[12]

She consulted soothsayers, experts on the interpretation of such dreams, who agreed with her that the dream held great significance. Many suggestions were offered, but Olympias strongly believed that the only real explanation was that she was pregnant, and that the child in her womb had been fathered by a god. It is not known whether she shared that idea with

Philip, and if she had, what the king's reaction might have been.

When the baby was born (most likely in July or August 356 B.C.), Philip was away with his army, waging a war against nearby Thrace. A messenger approached Philip's camp with three messages for the king. The first was that one of Philip's most able generals, Parmenio, had won a major battle in the west. The second item of news concerned the Olympic Games. Philip's race horse had come in first in an Olympic race, and that, too, pleased the king. The third message was that Olympias had given birth to a son, Alexander.

Three lucky pieces of news! Could this be a message from the gods? It was Philip's turn to consult the soothsayers, and Plutarch writes that "[they] raised his

Alexander with his mother Olympias, who had great ambitions for the young Alexander.

At First, a Marriage of Love

While many royal marriages in ancient times were marriages of convenience only, the union of Philip and Olympias began as a passionate love between two very independent individuals, as historian John Keegan writes in The Mask of Command.

"[Philip] took women where he found them, and, as he spent his life on the move and impressing his will on the world, the women were many and the outcome of his encounters with them unreckoned. But the marriage with Olympias was a love match, the love contracted at a celebration of certain mysterious . . . religious ceremonies held a year before Alexander's birth. . . . Olympias, already divorced, had no demure reputation and would not acquire one as time passed. Though she and Philip were soon to fall out, the attraction between them was probably that of equivalent, rather than complementary, spirits—wild, carnal, and contemptuous of convention. Both were of royal blood and neither, in an age when royalty claimed kinship with the gods, would have thought matchmakers . . . necessary intermediaries in what they felt for each other."

spirits still higher by assuring him that the son whose birth coincided with three victories would himself prove invincible."[13]

A Troubled Home

Although the birth of a son was joyous news, the royal home was not happy. Philip was busy making Macedon into a fearsome power in the ancient world, and his military ventures took him far from home most of the year. These long absences angered Olympias. But even when Philip was not fighting, he was having affairs with other women. Faithfulness in marriage was expected only of women in those days; men—in particular powerful

men such as King Philip—had no such limitations on their lives. Infidelity was not only expected among men, but was a sign of manliness.

But Olympias did not care what society expected or tolerated. Philip's actions infuriated her. Each rumor of another of his affairs added to her fury, and by the time Alexander was five or six, Olympias and Philip were open enemies.

Olympias used her time alone with her young son to remind the child of his immortal ancestors: Achilles on his mother's side, and Hercules on his father's. But, say historians, Olympias also told Alexander stories about the supernatural events she believed caused his birth—that although Philip was his earthly parent, he was most likely sired by a god. The stories probably

Born to the Sword

Olympias often told Alexander that his ancestor was the legendary hero Hercules.

confused and frightened the little boy. However, historian Mary Renault believes that by constantly reminding Alexander that Philip was the enemy, Olympias ensured that her little boy would remain loyal to her. "Hating her husband, [Olympias] wished wholly to possess her son."[14] Years later, when Alexander was forced to take sides in his parents' bickering, the early coaching he received from his mother would be painfully obvious.

Even with turmoil in his life, Alexander was a confident, bright little boy. He was reminded often of his heroic ancestors, and he believed that the great lives of Achilles and Hercules would inspire and direct his own. "As heir of Macedon," writes Mary Renault, "he was reared from his cradle in unquestioning acceptance of having been born to the sword, as a farmhand's son to the plow. Neither to Philip nor Olympias would any other future have been thinkable. It remained only to excel."[15]

The few remaining stories about Alexander's boyhood seem to illustrate his early interest in achieving such goals. One tells of a time when Alexander was about seven years old. A group of Persian diplomats had come to Macedon to see Philip; however, the king was off with his army fighting neighboring tribes. The diplomats were pleased to sit and talk with Alexander for a time.

They thought the boy would ply them with questions about far-off Persia. They expected to be asked about the wonders and sights—the ornate gardens hanging on arches in the air, or the palace of the king which glittered with precious jewels. But Alexander's questions were not the questions of a seven-year-old boy. After exchanging a few pleasantries, as historian Peter Green points out, Alexander "proceeded to grill his guests like any intelligence officer."

Not for him wide-eyed questions about such marvels as the Hanging Gardens or the Persian royal regalia. What *he* wanted to know were such things as the size and morale of the Persian army, the length of the journey to Susa [an important city in Persia], and the conditions of the roads that led there.[16]

"Macedon Is Too Small for You"

Another anecdote about Alexander shows not his keen interest in military affairs, but his self-confidence and boldness: two qualities necessary for a good general. The incident took place when the boy was ten or eleven years old, when Philip was considering buying a race horse. The horse was named Bucephalas, meaning "ox-head," because of an oxshaped mark on its forehead. Bucephalas's behavior did not please Philip at first.

> The king and his friends went down to the plain to watch the horse's trials and came to the conclusion that he was wild and quite unmanageable, for he would allow no one to mount him, nor would he endure the shouts of Philip's grooms, but reared up against anyone who approached him.[17]

Philip ordered the horse's owner to lead him away, for he had no interest in such an unruly animal. But Alexander, who had been watching the goings-on, interrupted his father. He remarked that Philip would be losing a great horse by sending the owner away, simply because no one knew how to handle the animal. Philip scoffed at Alexander's impertinence and chided his son for second-guessing his elders, reminding him that he could do no better. But Alexander disagreed, and declared that he could indeed manage the horse.

Philip was angry and embarrassed at the boy's boasts. He asked his son what penalty he would pay for his impertinence if he could not master the horse. Alexander replied that he would pay the entire price of the animal himself. According to historians, the crowd of men burst into laughter, for the idea that a little boy could manage such a large, wild horse was unthinkable.

But Alexander's self-confidence was well supported. He had noticed that Bucephalas seemed to shy from the sight of his own shadow, which moved whenever the horse did. Alexander turned the animal into the sun, so that the horse no longer saw the shadow and calmed down. When Alexander felt the horse relax, he

The young Alexander's taming of Bucephalas was a harbinger of his future greatness.

climbed onto its back, galloped around the pasture, and returned to his dumbfounded father.

"The rest of the company broke into loud applause," writes Plutarch, "while his father, we are told, wept for joy, and when Alexander had dismounted he kissed him and said, 'My boy, you must find a kingdom big enough for your ambitions. Macedon is too small for you.' "[18]

The Rugged Life

But Alexander needed more than horsemanship and self-confidence to be a good king. He needed discipline. Philip worried that Olympias spoiled the boy too much. Yet Philip was hardly the man to teach his son, for he was away most of the year on military adventures. To educate the future king, Philip hired a stern, tough tutor named Leonidas, an uncle of Olympias. Leonidas's job was to ensure that Alexander's life in Macedon was not the pampered life of a crown prince.

Leonidas did his job well. He put Alexander on a strict regimen, carefully monitoring his meals and exercise. Later Alexander would remember that Leonidas's idea of a healthy diet was "a night march to prepare for breakfast, and a moderate breakfast to curb an appetite for supper."[19]

Leonidas did not trust Olympias, for he suspected she tried to smuggle extra food in the boy's marching gear. "The man [Leonidas] himself used to come and look through my bedding boxes and clothes chests," Alexander wrote, "to see my mother did not hide any luxuries or extras there."[20]

Leonidas toughened the boy up, but Philip knew that Alexander needed more training than the old tutor could provide. Besides, having a relative of Queen Olympias as his son's teacher worried the king a bit. As the royal marriage became more and more unfriendly, Philip was concerned that Olympias's influence on her son would become too strong.

To counter these worries, Philip sent for a teacher who was probably the wisest man in all of Greece: Aristotle. At the tender age of thirteen, Alexander met the man who would profoundly affect the rest of his short life.

Alexander the Student

Aristotle had also been a student of a famous man: Plato, the most renowned thinker in the ancient Greek world. Aristotle was the author of between five hundred and a thousand books on an amazing range of topics, from biology, physics, music, and geometry, to medicine and astronomy. A master of many subjects, he came to Macedon to share his love of learning with the young prince Alexander. And although Philip remained a strong influence in his son's life, Alexander sometimes declared that he loved Aristotle as much as his father. "The one had given me life," said Alexander, "but the Philosopher [Aristotle] had shown me how to live well."[21]

So that Aristotle and his pupil could study without distraction, Philip arranged a retreat for them in Mieza, a rural section of Macedon that was far from the busy activity of the capital. There the two spent hours each day reading and talking. Aristotle's main love was philosophy, which in

Alexander with his tutor Aristotle, one of the most influential thinkers of the ancient world (left). Aristotle introduced Alexander to the writer Homer (below), whose epic poems thrilled and inspired the young student.

those days was central to all other studies. Philosophy today tends to concern itself with abstract shades of language and is very difficult for many people to follow, but in Alexander's day, the study of philosophy was quite basic. Writes historian Mary Renault:

> Its language was comprehensible to the lay ear and its subject was ultimate human value judgments. Its conclusions on these were brought to bear in debate upon law, statecraft, and personal ethics.[22]

In short, their discussions of philosophy laid the foundation for Alexander's ideas of what it meant to be a soldier and a king.

Alexander found these lessons immensely enjoyable. He was spellbound as Aristotle taught him principles of zoology and botany—so spellbound that years later on military campaigns, Alexander collected hundreds of plant and animal specimens to study and observe. He even banded stags, hoping to learn about their migration habits.

But the lessons Alexander enjoyed the most were of literature. Aristotle introduced the boy to the best poets and writers of the ancient world. Of all of these,

Alexander loved the work of Homer, who wrote *The Iliad*, the epic poem that told the story of the Trojan War. The tales of adventure, love, bravery, and loyalty excited Alexander and made him even more proud that he was related to the Greek war hero, Achilles.

Because his pupil so enjoyed Homer's work (and even memorized most of it), Aristotle presented Alexander with a

The World in Alexander's Day

What was known and understood about the continents of the world in the fourth century B.C. was far different from reality, as Maureen Ash explains in her book, Alexander the Great.

"If you compare a map of the world today to a map of the world the Greeks knew in 356 B.C., you begin to understand how little the people then knew about the earth. Only the Mediterranean Sea and the Italian and Greek peninsulas are in any sort of proportion. Europe is squeezed down to almost nothing, and the Iberian peninsula, occupied now by Spain and Portugal, is shown to be the same size as Italy. The great continent of Africa takes up only a small space and is called Libya. And Persia and India, the lands shown to the east of the Mediterranean, cover the areas we now call Iraq, Iran, Afghanistan, Pakistan, and India. Nothing was known then of the rest of the continent we still call Asia. Alexander and his teachers did not begin to guess at the millions of square miles that lay to the north and west of them as they studied geography in the palace at Pella, in Macedon."

personal copy of the poem. For the rest of his life, Alexander valued the book above other possessions. He carried it on every military campaign and even slept with it under his pillow.

The quiet times between student and teacher passed very quickly. After three years of tutoring (343-340 B.C.), Alexander's time in Mieza came to an end. Philip needed Alexander for more pressing matters, for the kingdom of Macedon was in jeopardy. Philip knew that if his son was to follow him as a general and ruler, he would need to be trained in more violent arts, and the time for learning these skills was at hand.

Chapter

2 From Soldier to King

While Alexander was learning from Aristotle, King Philip was busy extending the borders of Macedon. Though reading about battles and wars had taught Alexander a great deal about history and sparked a great interest in military matters, he had never had any firsthand experience as a soldier. In this area of study, Philip himself would be Alexander's teacher.

Philip's armies were successful for several reasons. For one thing, Philip was a good leader, a brave general who was trusted by his men. In the fourth century B.C., wars were fought very differently than modern wars. Battles were fought and won by the soldiers who could shoot arrows or slings more accurately, or who could use spears more viciously. As historian Jacob Abbott observes, things were far different in the ancient world, where "headlong bravery and muscular force were the qualities that generally carried the day."[23]

Those same qualities applied to generals. Unlike generals of the modern age, who are strategists and planners, generals of that era fought in the front lines alongside their men. Philip had never been afraid to join his infantry in battle, and his appearance proved his courage. "Few bore so many battle scars as Philip," writes one

King Philip loses an eye in battle. His great courage prompted one historian to note that "few bore so many battle scars as Philip."

historian. "An old wound made him limp, a broken collarbone still pained him; and one of his eyes had been gouged from its socket."[24]

But there was a bigger reason for Philip's military success: one which young Alexander had to study if he was to lead the Macedonian army someday. Philip brought brilliant innovations to his army—methods never before tried in any of the Greek states that considered themselves on the cutting edge of civilization. Philip's innovations paved the way not only for his own victories, but also for the future triumphs of his son.

Hoplites, Pikes, and National Pride

Before Philip's innovations, the infantry soldier, called a *hoplite*, was the backbone of the army. The hoplite was a foot soldier, armed with a sword, a large wooden shield trimmed in copper, and an eight-foot-long spear. There were also cavalry who fought on horseback, but these were not as important or effective as hoplites in battle. Stirrups had not yet been invented, and it was very difficult for all but the best bareback horsemen to maneuver a large horse and use a sword or lance at the same time.

Hoplites were arranged into a large formation called a phalanx, the Greek word for "finger." A phalanx was a unit of soldiers eight or ten rows deep. The soldiers in a phalanx stood shoulder to shoulder, spears pointed out, shields up. The unit marched quickly ahead to attack, and when they were on the defensive, they stood in a square.

The system worked fairly well for the Greeks, but Philip made some changes that placed the Macedonians at an advantage. First of all, he enlarged the Macedonian army phalanx formation. Hoplites were arranged in rows of sixteen men.

Ancient Greek warriors armed themselves with spears, short swords, and wooden shields.

King Philip shaped the Macedonian army into an aggressive fighting force.
His innovations included the invention of the sarissa, *a sixteen-foot-long pike.*

Philip replaced the eight-foot-long spears with a new invention called a *sarissa*, a sixteen-foot-long pike. Hoplites carrying sarissas reached their targets faster than soldiers with spears half as long; the sarissas were so long, that those carried by men in the fourth row of the phalanx protruded over the shoulders of those in the front row! In a defensive stance, the phalanx was as impenetrable as a gigantic porcupine.

Philip also varied his phalanx from the Greek form by giving the men more space between their lines. Instead of marching shoulder to shoulder, as though forming a human wall, they had ten or twelve inches of space between them. This allowed the soldiers much more maneuverability in their marches.

Philip's army differed from Greek armies in another important respect. The Greek armies were largely composed of thousands of mercenaries, foreigners hired to fight battles for the Greeks. Mercenaries were professional soldiers and seasoned fighters. At the beginning of his reign, Philip did not have the money to hire mercenaries, for Macedon's treasury was not as rich as the city-states of Greece. At the same time, he wanted soldiers as skilled and as capable as these foreign professionals.

Philip's answer was to create a national army. His soldiers went through intensive drilling, enduring week-long marches up and down steep hills carrying heavy packs and weapons. The result of such brutal

Alexander astride the mighty Bucephalas. The two were inseparable throughout Alexander's meteoric career.

training was a fighting force that was so conditioned that it could attack, in perfect synchronization, on a dead run. The men could race hundreds of yards carrying close to one hundred pounds of armor, supplies, and weapons. This new Macedonian army was Philip's pride and joy and would be a legacy to his son.

First Taste of Battle

Since his ascent to the throne, Philip had continued to subdue his enemies with his army, and for the most part, the Greek states were yielding to his authority. However, some people in Athens and Thebes still considered Philip and the Macedonians barbarians and refused to fall into line behind him. It was against the united armies of Thebes and Athens that seventeen-year-old Alexander experienced his first battle.

The armies met in August 338 B.C. near Chaeronea, a village in central Greece. Philip had brought an infantry of thirty thousand men; the Greeks outnumbered them by five thousand. Each army also had approximately two thousand mounted cavalry fighters. As dawn approached on the morning of battle, both armies were given last-minute instructions.

Philip would command the right wing of the army; Alexander, mounted on Bucephalas, would lead the Companions, the most devoted of the king's followers, in a cavalry charge on the left side. As one historian notes, Philip had second thoughts about placing his teenage son in a position of such authority, "but he endeavored to guard against the danger of an unfortunate result by putting the ablest generals on Alexander's side, while he reserved those on whom he could place less reliance for his own."[25]

While he had confidence in his army, Philip knew that he should fear a special group of fighters from Thebes called the Sacred Band. These were the cream of the army, the best fighters in Thebes. The band was made up of pairs of friends who swore oaths to one another, and to their king, that they would die rather than surrender. They had never before lost a battle.

As both generals expected, the battle was long and bloody. The ancient historian Diodorus writes that "[it] was hotly contested for a long time, and many fell on both sides, so that for a while the struggle permitted hopes of victory to both; corpses piled up."[26] But in the end, Alexander's nerve and aggressive leadership, as well as Philip's perfect battle plan, won the battle of Chaeronea for Macedon.

Alexander and the Companions drove back the Theban soldiers as Philip's right wing pretended to be frightened by the charging Athenians. As Philip's wing fell back, the Athenians charged faster and faster. But it was a trap. After the Theban line finally snapped, the young prince suddenly wheeled his troops around toward the center. "Meanwhile," relates one historian, "Philip had drawn the Athenians on the right into a trap of low ground. Turn-

ing, Philip's wing smashed through the enemy's extended force and it too retreated toward the center."[27]

The Greek forces had been lulled into the jaws of a steel trap—Alexander and his Companions on one side, and Philip's crackerjack infantry on the other. Thousands of Athenians and Thebans were slaughtered, cut to pieces by the sharp swords and sarissas of the Macedonians. Even the three hundred members of the Sacred Band were no match for Alexander and his father; they fought bravely but were killed, too.

Philip's confidence in his son had paid off, for Alexander not only survived the battle, but also impressed soldiers far more experienced than he with his leadership and bravery. Plutarch writes that "because of these achievements . . . [he] became extravagantly fond of his son, so much so that he took pleasure in hearing the Macedonians speak of Alexander as their king and Philip as their general."[28]

Mercy, and a Plan

According to an old saying, one can do almost anything with bayonets except sit on them. In other words, one cannot successfully sit on a throne when one's power comes solely from military might. Philip was too intelligent to think he could rule all of Greece by relying on the muscle of his army—he did not have enough men to leave behind in all the places he conquered.

So while the news of the slaughter at Chaeronea traveled back to the Greek states and made the Athenians frantic with worry over what Philip would do to them, the Macedonian king surprised them all. To Athens, the most influential of all the Greek states, Philip showed "an astonishing generosity," writes historian A.R. Burn, "and saw to it that it was well publicized."[29] He allowed the Athenian prisoners to return home and did not even demand a ransom. Athens was instructed to become an ally of Macedon, but with the assurance from Philip that no Macedonian troops would occupy Athens.

Although he was not as merciful to the Thebans (Thebes was not as important to Philip's future plans) the people of Athens were impressed, and became even more so when he returned the ashes of their dead for proper burial. Instead of feeling defiance or outrage because their armies had been conquered by the "barbarians from

A Visit to Diogenes

In Stephen Krensky's book Conqueror and Hero, *he writes of a meeting between the twenty-year-old Alexander and an eccentric Greek named Diogenes. As he explains, the meeting left quite an impression on Alexander.*

"While in Corinth, Alexander visited the philosopher Diogenes, whom he had heard much about. Diogenes was an unusual man. He lived as simply as possible, sometimes wearing a barrel instead of clothes. The tale is told that he once walked through the crowded city at night with a lantern, searching for one honest man. Such a figure intrigued Alexander. He found Diogenes sitting on the ground, thinking. The philosopher did not rise as the king's shadow stretched across him. Alexander introduced himself and offered to grant Diogenes a request. The philosopher had only one—that the king step aside to let the sunshine reach him. Alexander took no offense. While his companions laughed at Diogenes' sour manner, Alexander admired him for his steadfast beliefs. Supposedly, he even said, 'Were I not Alexander, I would wish to be Diogenes.'"

Alexander visits the eccentric Diogenes.

Macedon," most Greeks felt respect for Philip. When he called for a gathering of representatives of all the Greek states to be held in Corinth, every district attended except Sparta, and those at the meeting listened with interest to his plan.

Philip's dream was not limited to the control of Greece. In reality, his activities in Greece—forming alliances through negotiations or force, and now the formation of the League of Corinth—were merely the groundwork for his true ambition, which was to invade Persia, a huge kingdom to the east. Persia was an enemy to both Macedon and Greece, for Persia's General Xerxes had invaded Greece in 480 B.C., almost one hundred fifty years earlier. Although the Greeks eventually had rallied and defeated the Persians, the invasion had infuriated the Greeks. Combining their forces under King Philip of Macedon to seek revenge on the Persian Empire was a pleasing thought.

Philip's success in Greece became more and more evident. He was the undisputed head of the League of Corinth and the unanimous choice to lead troops into Persia. Although Olympias had tried to exert complete control over her son, the beginning of a solid bond between Alexander and his father had seemed to appear. But something shattered that bond completely, forever souring relations between the two.

A Bitter Quarrel

Philip decided in 337 B.C. to marry again. This was not at all uncommon at the time—Philip already had six wives, counting Olympias. His new love was a woman named Cleopatra, the beautiful young daughter of a Macedonian nobleman. Historians say that this marriage differed from Philip's others because he married for love, rather than for political convenience.

Her husband's plans to add another wife enraged Olympias. She saw Cleopatra as a rival: because Cleopatra was Macedonian, any son she might have could be considered a more rightful heir to the throne than Alexander when Philip died. As she had done many times before, Olympias held long conferences with her son, urging him to oppose his father in such a marriage.

But the views of Alexander and his mother mattered not at all to King Philip, and tempers reached the boiling point at the wedding feast. Cleopatra's uncle Attalus, a general in the Macedonian army, had too much to drink and proposed a toast that directly insulted Alexander and Olympias. He hoped that the gods would bless the marriage and give Philip and Cleopatra a legitimate heir to the throne. According to Plutarch, Alexander

> flew into a rage at these words and shouted at him, "Villain, do you take me for a bastard, then?" and hurled a drinking cup at his head. At this Philip lurched to his feet, and drew his sword against his son, but fortunately for them both he was so overcome with drink and with rage that he tripped and fell headlong.
>
> Alexander jeered at him and cried out, "Here is the man who was making ready to cross from Europe to Asia, and who cannot even cross from one table to another without losing his balance."[30]

Alexander left the hall in a rage, took Olympias, and angrily left for Illyria, northwest of Macedon.

Unrest in Macedon

So began a dark, uneasy time in Macedon. Currents of hostility and unrest created distrust and suspicion among the nobles and the army. Was Alexander gone for good? Was Cleopatra, now pregnant, carrying the next king of Macedon? While Philip brooded about the humiliation his son had caused him, and Olympias conferred with her son about their next move, Alexander's future seemed very bleak indeed.

Philip might never have seen Alexander again if not for the advice of a friend, Demaratus from Corinth. Demaratus had come to Macedon to see Philip, and the king asked him for news of the Greek states. Were they in harmony with one another, or had they returned to their habit of squabbling and fighting?

Demaratus replied in a stern manner, "It is all very well for you to show so much concern for the affairs of Greece, Philip. How about the disharmony you have brought about in your own household?" According to Plutarch, "this reply sobered Philip to such an extent that he sent for Alexander, and with Demaratus's help persuaded him to return."[31]

Though Alexander returned to the palace along with his mother, there were bitter feelings. Alexander was still unsure of his status in the royal hierarchy. Was he still a crown prince of Macedon, destined for the throne? Or was Philip waiting for Cleopatra to give birth to a son of pure Macedonian blood? The answers unfolded in a bloody series of events during the summer of 336 B.C. And as before, the backdrop for the drama was a wedding.

This time one of Philip's daughters was to be married to a foreign noble, and Philip was making a grand display of his power. This was an occasion to show off, for he was commander of the joint forces of the League of Corinth. On the day of the wedding, in fact, an advance force of ten thousand troops led by his trusted general Parmenio was marching into Asia Minor to lay the groundwork for a future invasion. Also, during the preparations for the grand wedding, his wife Cleopatra had given birth to a son. It was a time of celebration.

A grand procession took place in the morning, during which statues of the gods were carried into the hall. Perhaps to hint that he considered himself on the same level as the Greek gods, Philip added a statue of himself to the group. As he walked into the hall, Philip walked alone, away from his usual crowd of bodyguards, for "he wanted to show publicly that he was protected by the goodwill of all the Greeks, and had no need of a guard of spearmen."[32] No armed guards hovered over him; he did not need them. He was loved and respected by his people, and was perfectly at ease.

But the display of courage that morning cost Philip his life. As he made his way into the hall, nodding and talking to supporters and guests, one of the bodyguards rushed at him. Pulling a short hunting knife from under his shirt, the man plunged it deep into the king's back. Philip died instantly.

Meanwhile, the rest of the bodyguards chased the killer. As historian Peter Green writes,

> He eluded his pursuers until, getting on to his waiting horse, he tripped over a vine; whereupon the rest of the bodyguards fell upon him with javelins, saving him from gruesome torture. But

Olympias a Murderer?

Some ancient as well as modern historians are convinced that Olympias was the one who planned her husband's death. In Peter Green's book Alexander the Great, *he writes about her suspicious behavior after the deaths of Philip and Pausanias.*

"'Most of the blame,' says Plutarch, 'devolved upon Olympias, on the ground that she had added her exhortations to the young man's anger and incited him to the deed.' Her subsequent behavior, indeed, suggests that she not only planned her husband's death, but openly gloried in it—perhaps as a means of diverting suspicion from Alexander himself, who, after all, benefited more by Pausanias's action than anyone. The murderer's corpse was nailed to a public gibbet [gallows]; that very same night Olympias placed a gold crown on its head. A few days later she had the body taken down, burnt it over Philip's ashes, and buried it in a nearby grave. Every year she poured libations there on the anniversary of the murder."

he was dead before any information could be got out of him about the other plotters in the [assassination].[33]

Mystery surrounds Philip's death, even in modern times. The "who" is no mystery—the assassin was named Pausanias. The "why" is more difficult. Historians disagree as to Pausanias's motive. Some say he had been passed over for promotions in court; others contend he had been sexually assaulted by some nobles, perhaps even by King Philip himself. But some historians, while not denying these motives, also suggest that Olympias herself might have been behind the plot. Plutarch wrote that "[Olympias] was believed to have encouraged the young man and incited him to take his revenge."[34]

No one will ever know for certain to what extent Olympias was involved in her husband's murder. But twenty-year-old Alexander had more pressing problems than solving that mystery, and the most important task was to secure the throne he so desperately wanted.

Bremen High School
Media Center

3 Establishing Command

Although the Macedonian government was a monarchy, certain stipulations applied to the transfer of power. In most circumstances, the king's son took over the throne, but not until the army had given him a vote of confidence. Alexander's status was shaky. Cleopatra had produced an

Alexander's image captured in stone by the Greek sculptor Lysippus.

infant son, whom some might consider a logical heir to the throne. There were also often-repeated rumors (sometimes even spread by Olympias herself) that Philip was not Alexander's true father. Obtaining a vote of confidence from the army was not something Alexander could take for granted.

"Nothing Has Changed"

However, Alexander showed tremendous leadership within moments of the announcement of Philip's death, reassuring Macedonians who might have felt frightened and panicky. "He called upon the people to be calm and undismayed," writes one historian. "All things would be administered exactly as under his father. 'Nothing,' he ended, 'has changed, except the name of the king.'"[35]

An official assembly was held to determine whether his unofficial—but very obvious—claim to the throne would be upheld. In Macedon the candidates for king stood in front of the group. Army officials wore their armor, and when the name of the candidate they liked was read, they showed their support by clashing their spears against their breastplates. Historian

An Ancient Feud

Historians have long disagreed on what Alexander's goals were as he set off toward Asia Minor. As John Keegan writes in The Mask of Command, *the king had a great deal of support for an all-out war against the Persians.*

"Alexander's real purpose from the outset of his reign was to invade the Persian empire. How far he initially intended his invasion to go is still debated. It was enough for his Greek contemporaries that he intended to go at all. Persia, the most powerful state in the known world, stretching from the Mediterranean to the Indian Ocean, permanently menaced and had twice invaded Greece. But Greek antipathy for Persia was based not merely on menace and military history. Greek states were frequently at war with each other; indeed Greek political theory held the 'state of war' to be the normal relationship between neighbors. The feeling of Greeks towards Persians, however, was harsher than that. Free Greeks feared and hated the Persians as instruments of a despotic power bent on robbing them of liberty and reducing them to subject status. A war against Persia therefore partook of the character of 'crusade', and Alexander, as war leader, of the role of his civilization's champion."

John Keegan points out that such a display was "a sign of their readiness to shed the blood of their challengers."[36]

Although Cleopatra's tiny son was too young to command the army, some nobles believed that even Alexander was too young: that an older, more experienced general should be appointed king, at least until there was a clearer choice. But Alexander had the support of two of Philip's most trusted generals, Antipater and Parmenio. They trusted Alexander, and said so. Even more impressive were the shouts of support from the fighting men, who had seen Alexander in action on the battlefield. To them, Alexander would be a king worthy of their respect.

The clanking of spears upon armor in that assembly was, to Alexander, the sweetest music in the world.

Even so, precautions—certainly brutal by today's standards—had to be taken. As Keegan writes, "The culling of rivals and the execution of enemies of the regime . . . was common practice in Alexander's world, a policy of prudence in a society where the sword spoke more mightily than the law."[37] It was necessary to eliminate those Macedonians who might pose a threat to the new king. Generals who might plot his death, or nobles who were outspoken in their criticism of Alexander were executed. Olympias herself participated in the purge, according to ancient historians. She is said to have thrown Cleopatra's newborn baby into a sacrificial fire, causing Cleopatra so much grief that she later hanged herself.

Joy in Greece

While the people of Macedon mourned Philip's death, the Greeks celebrated in the streets. The end of Philip, they felt, was the end of Macedon's power. No

Following Philip's death, Demosthenes fueled anti-Macedon sentiment by urging the Greek states to oppose Alexander.

longer would they have to lend financial and military support to the League of Corinth, which Philip had captained. The embarrassment of having a "barbarian" in charge of the combined forces of Greece was a thing of the past.

In Athens, the anti-Macedon sentiment was especially strong. Demosthenes, a longtime critic of Philip, gave a public speech praising the assassin Pausanias. He urged Athens and the other Greek states to disband the league, and even encouraged the armed uprisings against Macedon which were beginning in Thebes.

Thessaly, Thrace, Thebes, and other states agreed with Demosthenes. Although they did not really know Alexander, they did not respect him. In their eyes he was too young to be any sort of threat to them. He could never carry on his father's plans to invade Persia, and therefore there was no reason to maintain the League of Corinth. So the league collapsed, nullifying Philip's hard work.

When he heard the reports of the Greek rebellion, Alexander was enraged. His instinct was to march southward, through the Greek states, and prove that he was as worthy of respect as his father had been. Advisors to the king tried to calm him, urging him not to be too rash in his actions.

But Alexander would not listen. According to Plutarch, the young king decided that "the only way to make his kingdom safe was to act with audacity and a lofty spirit, for he was certain that if he were seen to yield even a fraction of his authority, all his enemies would attack him at once."[38] There were even rumors that tribes to the north (long subdued by Philip) were preparing for war against Macedon. Alexander had no interest in waiting to see what others would do. He intended to follow Philip's plan of taking revenge on Persia. Without the backing and participation of the Greeks, it would never happen. He and his army would march south immediately.

A Victory and a Prophecy

The victory was surprisingly easy—some historians have even speculated that Alexander must have been disappointed that the fight was little more than a skirmish. He and his armies marched first into Thessaly, experiencing little resistance from the people there. After adding valuable cavalry troops from Thessaly to his own army, Alexander moved quickly into Corinth. Again, the Greeks were so startled by the aggression that they wasted no time in surrendering. A meeting of the league was hastily called, and with the exception of Sparta, the representatives meekly agreed to support the league. Historian Mercer writes that "the federation members promised to be peaceful, named Alexander their captain-general, and no doubt expressed relief among themselves when he made plans to lead his army quietly back to Macedon."[39]

Before returning to Macedon to plan his Persian campaign, Alexander decided to stop in Delphi to participate in a tradition which even then was considered ancient. In Delphi was a temple to the god Apollo, who, people believed, spoke prophecies to those who visited. A high priestess, known as a Pythia, would sit on a three-legged stool above a sacred flame. The flame, which gave off a pungent aroma, excited the Pythia and caused her to

The priestess over the sacred flame at Delphi. To Alexander, she prophesied, "My son, thou art invincible!"

rave and babble incoherently. A priest of Apollo would translate the gibberish for the visitor.

Alexander wanted desperately to know if his upcoming military invasion would be successful, and he needed reassurance from the Pythia. However, he arrived at Delphi on a day when, according to the temple priests, the conditions were unfavorable for a prophecy. Although he insisted that he be permitted to talk to the Pythia, the priests refused him.

But Alexander was not a man to be denied. With the impatience and aggressiveness that were becoming his trademark, he marched to the home of the Pythia and asked her directly. It is not certain how he convinced her to give him a prophecy. "Possibly he responded with good-natured flattery," writes one historian, "for he had a charming way with elderly women. Or perhaps . . . Alexander drew her into the temple by force. At any rate, she finally gave him an answer—'My son, thou art invincible!'"[40] Alexander was satisfied that his future was promising and headed back to Macedon, where urgent business awaited him.

The Longest Spear

The foot soldiers of the Macedonian army under Philip and Alexander relied on the longest spear ever used, the sarissa. As Robin Lane Fox writes in The Search For Alexander, *the addition of sarissas changed the entire form of the army.*

"In the center, the tribal foot battalions were given an unusual look. They were based on an original depth of ten and were newly formed up with their famous sarissas. These tough spears of cornel wood were riveted together to a length of sixteen feet. They had to be held with two hands, though a long butt spike and a thin spearhead of metal helped to balance them. Thinner than the medieval pike, the long sarissas projected in a bristling wall beyond the first few ranks of the formation. Their bearers were trained to swish them up and down when advancing rapidly. Terrified opponents compared the effect to spikes on a giant porcupine. Others, perhaps Philip himself, compared it with Homer's Greek army before Troy."

The sight of the bristling Macedonian phalanx must have been bone chilling.

The Macedonian phalanx beats back Thracian troops in a battle that would prove Alexander's value as a general.

Fighting Creatively

In Macedon, the nobles were in an uproar. The Thracians, Celts, and other tribes were stirring up trouble in the north, for precisely the same reasons as the Greeks: they thought Alexander would be unable to do anything about it. It was January and there would be no armed conflict for weeks, as no fighting occurred during the winter months. But as soon as the spring thaws began in 335 B.C., an eager Alexander led his troops northeast, to the first real battle since assuming the throne.

He encountered a Thracian patrol blocking a narrow mountain pass—the only way from Macedon into their mountainous country. It was here that Alexander fought his first real battle and, according to historians, showed his value as a general. Time after time, in his short but active years as general and king, he saved lives with his quick thinking. His resourcefulness and creativity consistently strengthened his army, and improved its odds in situations where the Macedonians were clearly the underdog.

In this case, the Thracians on the ridge near the top of the mountain pass had heavy wooden wagons. The soldiers used the wagons to form a stockade in case of attack. But according to the ancient historian Arrian, the wagons had another, more aggressive function.

> It was also in their mind to launch the carts at the Macedonian Phalanx as the troops mounted the slope just where the mountain was most precipitous. Their idea was that the closer packed the phalanx when the descending carts charged it, the more their violent descent would scatter it.[41]

The Macedonian troops, climbing up the rugged trail while struggling with heavy weapons, must have thought they were in terrible danger. The heavy wagons, if sent crashing down the ridge, would crush them, or at the very least, would force their precise phalanx to break rank, which alone would put them at a disadvantage.

But Alexander had a plan. He told his men that when they heard him give a certain command, they were to part rank to the left and right. If they did it in order, the phalanx would split into two units, but each would stay tightly packed. The soldiers on rockier, less maneuverable ground would drop down and hold their large shields above them. When linked, the shields of the soldiers would form a tough roof, over which the wagons could roll without harming the men.

The plan worked perfectly. Unharmed by the wagons, the Macedonian army was able to gain control of the strategic mountain pass and rout the startled Thracians, who were ill prepared for an attack.

Crossing the Danube

Alexander's resourcefulness served him and his men well in the following battle. A tribe of Celtic rebels were camped on the far side of the Ister River, which is now known as the Danube. Never had the Macedonians seen such a deep, wild river. The small ships which Alexander had requested from the Macedonian navy were woefully unequal to the task of transporting the army—only ten to twenty men could fit in a boat at one time. At that rate, Alexander's army would take days to cross the river, and the handful of soldiers who were first to make the trip would be at the mercy of the Celts on the other side.

As the Celts kept watch from across the river, they were probably jeering at the Macedonians, whose best chance seemed to be to march dozens of miles downriver to find a shallower crossing. But that was time wasted, as far as Alexander was concerned. That evening he came up with a plan. According to Arrian, "he filled the leather tent-covers with hay, collected as many as possible of the boats from the countryside made from single tree trunks (they were plentiful, for the riverside dwellers used them for fishing) . . . and ferried across as much of his force as he could in this way."[42] According to the same source, about fifteen hundred cavalry and four thousand infantry soldiers crossed the Ister River this way in the dead of night.

The Celts were paralyzed with fright the next morning when Alexander led a charge against them. Many threw down their weapons, thinking that this army was somehow superhuman, for how else could such a mass of men cross so quickly? The victory was easy, and again resourcefulness on Alexander's part had made heavy fighting unnecessary. His hoplites and cavalry sustained only minor injuries and were in good form to fight another day.

Alexander gained something else with victory over the Celts. The Celts repeated the story of the Macedonians' mysterious ability to cross over water to other tribes. Rather than waiting for Alexander and his forces, these tribes sent diplomats to his camp to plead for peace. During his reign, Alexander would have no further trouble from his northerly neighbors.

A False Report

While Alexander and his armies were busy in the north, his old rival Demosthenes was stirring up trouble in the south. A rumor that Alexander had been killed in a battle began to circulate, and the story triggered joy and celebration in Greece, similar to the reaction when King Philip died. It is not certain that Demosthenes started the rumor, but the Athenian statesman certainly capitalized on it. As one historian writes, "To make this [rumor] more plausible, he produced the messenger, bandaged and bloody, who swore he had received his wounds in the same battle."[43]

After "proving" that Alexander was dead, Demosthenes gave public speeches urging the Greek states to regain their pride and cast off the influence of Macedon. Although sparks of rebellion began flickering in many Greek states, the largest movement came from Thebes. There, great armies began to mobilize for a confrontation with the Macedonians.

It did not take long for word of this trouble to reach Alexander in the north. He heard that Demosthenes was encouraging armed rebellion and was even sending money and weapons to Thebes to help the revolt. But what outraged Alexander most was Demosthenes' involvement with the Persians—people who were supposedly the Greeks' mortal enemies. The Persian king Darius was obviously interested in the League of Corinth, for if that federation were strong, Persia would be threatened. It was in Darius's best interests to keep the Greek states from acting in unison.

Under normal conditions, the Persian government did not involve itself in the affairs of Greece. But according to historian Peter Green, "the Great King [Darius] had, at long last, reversed his earlier policy of non-interference, and was now channeling gold into Greece wherever he thought it would do most good. The mere thought . . . must have turned Alexander's blood cold."[44]

The Slaughter of Thebes

Alexander knew he had no choice but to march his army south, to Thebes, to restore order there. If reports were accurate, the Theban army was well armed and ready to do battle with Macedon, and had the support of not only the Greek states, but also professional mercenaries.

Quick action had helped Alexander in the past, and it served him this time as well. In an unheard-of display of energy and endurance, Alexander and his troops marched three hundred miles in just two weeks. (In those days, a march of twenty miles over rough terrain in one day was

Fearing Greek revolt, Alexander and his army stormed into Thebes and demolished the city. The massacre was more vicious and bloody than any the ancient world had seen.

The Appearance of a King

In John Keegan's book The Mask of Command, *the author explains that Alexander was unmistakable in battle. His armor and garments were intended to draw attention, rather than keep him camouflaged and safe from enemy archers and foot soldiers.*

"For an encounter with the enemy he dressed in a special and conspicuous style. Leaders of a later age—Frederick the Great, Napoleon . . . Wellington, Grant—affected an unostentatious appearance, but theirs was a style of leadership reflective and managerial rather than heroic; they were to 'lead' from the rear. Alexander, who led in the precise sense of the word, needed to be seen and to be recognized instantaneously, and he dressed accordingly. 'His helmet,' Curtius tells us, 'was of iron but so polished that it shone like the brightest silver; of its lofty, graceful crest, the nodding plumes were remarkable for their snowy whiteness. His body armor was formed of double layers of linen, strongly quilted; a throat-piece of iron, enriched with sparkling gems, connected this with the helmet. From a superb belt hung a sword famed for edge and temper . . . it was light and easy to wield. . . .' Over all, he slung a magnificent cloak and usually he had carried near him the sacred armour he had taken from the temple of Athena at Troy, reputed to be relics of the Trojan War."

considered an accomplishment.) When the Thebans heard a rumor that Alexander was approaching, they had two reasons to disbelieve it: Alexander was supposedly dead, and, if he weren't dead, it would have been impossible for any army to cover so much ground so quickly.

But the disbelief changed to fear, at least for some of the people of Thebes. They had no wish to fight this amazing Macedonian army. Alexander sensed that his unexpected appearance had given him a momentary advantage, and he announced to the Thebans that they had a chance to join the Macedonians before it

was too late. Writes Plutarch, "He wished to give the citizens the opportunity to repent of their actions, and so he merely demanded the surrender of their leaders . . . and offered an amnesty to all the rest if they would come over to his side."[45]

Some of the Thebans might have responded to his offer, but they were dissuaded by their leaders. Alexander received word that the Thebans wanted war, not amnesty. They were fighting for the pride of the Greek world. Angrily, the Macedonian king vowed the Thebans would pay dearly for their treachery and stupidity.

Many historians consider the battle at Thebes one of the bloodiest of the ancient world. Although the Thebans thought they were prepared for war, they were no match for the enraged Macedonians. As Alexander's troops burst through the city gates, a savage massacre ensued. Historian Jacob Abbott explains that the suspense of waiting outside the city for the fighting to begin excited Alexander's men to a frenzied pitch:

> Soldiers under such circumstances, cannot be restrained and no imagination can conceive the horrors of the sacking of a city, carried by assault. . . . Tigers do not spring upon their prey with greater ferocity than man springs . . . to the perpetration of every possible cruelty upon his fellow man. . . . To plunder, burn, destroy, and kill, are the lighter and more harmless of the crimes they perpetrate.[46]

Arrian, writing from eyewitness accounts, writes that the Macedonians killed

> in hot blood . . . without restraint, even when [the Thebans] no longer offered resistance, some in their houses, which they broke into, some showing fight; others actually suppliant [praying] at the shrines—they spared neither woman nor child.[47]

Actually, a report claims that one woman was spared, and the story gives an odd twist to the brutality shown by Alexander in the accounts of the battle. As the victorious Macedonians were deciding which Theban civilians to execute and which to sell as slaves, two soldiers brought a Theban woman to Alexander. She was, they claimed, responsible for murdering one of the Macedonian soldiers. As she was led to Alexander, the woman looked, says Plutarch, to be "a woman of dignity and spirit."[48]

She did not deny she killed the soldier. He had raped her, the woman said, and afterwards demanded that she give him all her gold and silver. The woman pointed to a deep well, and told the soldier that she had thrown her jewelry down into it before the battle began, just in case. As the soldier leaned over to look into the well, she pushed him in and pelted him with heavy rocks until he was dead.

She also told Alexander that she was the daughter of a general, the same man who had commanded the Theban army against Philip in the battle at Chaeronea. When the woman finished speaking, the Macedonian troops no doubt felt certain that Alexander would enjoy executing her himself, but he surprised everyone. Plutarch explains that, "Alexander was filled with admiration not only at her words, but at what she had done, and gave orders that she and her children should be freed and allowed to depart."[49]

Apologies

As word of the slaughter at Thebes arrived in other Greek states, panic ensued. What now? Alexander would be furious with them, and quite possibly was making plans to march against their cities, too. With their customary flexibility, the Greek leaders sent messengers to Alexander, begging his forgiveness and pledging their undying loyalty.

But just as he had surprised his men by sparing the life of the Theban woman, Alexander probably astonished the Greeks. His father had recognized the need to keep Athens a strong, supportive ally, and

Alexander was a man of many legends, one of which illustrates his dual nature: During the slaughter at Thebes, a defiant Theban woman killed one of Alexander's officers (left). Amidst the screams of tortured and dying Thebans, Alexander confronted the woman, and, in a strange act of kindness, set her free (right).

Alexander did the same. He accepted the apologies and pledges of all of the Greeks, including the Athenians. And although he could have demanded heavy punishments for the Greek leaders who had betrayed him, he had only one score to settle—one with Demosthenes. He asked that the Athenian be banished forever from public life: punishment enough for a man whose life was centered on politics.

The battle at Thebes was fresh in people's minds; the Greeks did not wish to cross Alexander again. With the League of Corinth strong and the Greek leaders firmly behind him, Alexander returned home to begin planning the invasion of Persia. As he told his men, he intended to march east the following spring. And as history would show, he would never return to Macedon again.

Chapter

4 Taking On Persia

Alexander spent the winter months of 335-334 B.C. in Macedon, planning his springtime campaign: a full military invasion of Persia. He repeated to his colleagues that his motive was revenge. Hadn't the Persians themselves invaded Greece, laying waste to temples and homes? It was time for the Greeks (he included Macedonians, for they had fought shoulder to shoulder with their southern neighbors against the invaders from the East) to pay back the Persians. The Greek

cities in Asia that had been overtaken by Persia would be freed.

However, many historians believe that revenge was only a part of Alexander's plans. They maintain that Alexander was thinking bigger. He had no intentions of stopping after he liberated a few cities along the eastern coast of the Aegean Sea. He was lured by the adventure of taking on a monstrously large, wealthy kingdom—the most powerful in the ancient world at the time. Just as for Philip before

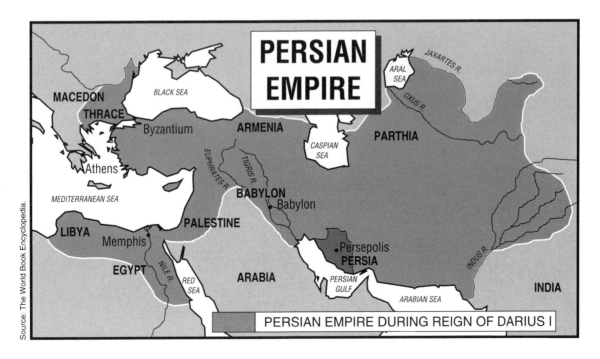

Source: The World Book Encyclopedia.

PERSIAN EMPIRE

PERSIAN EMPIRE DURING REIGN OF DARIUS I

him, avenging the few cities was Alexander's excuse for a greater military adventure: the conquest of the entire Persian Empire. As biographer W.W. Tarn explains, "He never thought of not doing it; it was his inheritance."[50]

Almost Unimaginable

The task, however, was almost impossible to imagine. The Persian Empire covered a vast area, across Asia as far east as India, north as far as the Caspian Sea, and as far south as Egypt—a region as large as the continental United States.

The empire had been founded two centuries before by Cyrus I, but it was Cyrus's successor, Darius I, who was responsible for the empire's expansion and strength. Darius had used his armies to acquire enormous amounts of territory, but had been wise enough to realize that he needed the cooperation of his subjects if he were to be a successful ruler. Simply possessing a mighty army was not enough to ensure control in such a large empire.

Unlike many kings, who insisted that their subjects conform in every way to their own customs, Darius was more than willing to use the languages, technologies, and cultures of the millions of people he ruled. This tolerance enabled him to administrate his empire with surprisingly little hostility from the people. As one historian points out, "Darius did not want revolt, he wanted money. And taxes were much easier to collect in peacetime."[51]

It was more than tolerance, however, that kept the vast Persian Empire together. Darius had divided the kingdom into

Cyrus the Great once ruled the vast Persian Empire.

King Darius with conquered rebels. Darius was a strong and ambitious ruler. Under his leadership, the Persian Empire was wealthy and powerful.

twenty individual districts, each under the supervision of a governor called a *satrap*. It was the job of each satrap to establish laws and levy taxes in his district. Because Darius was concerned that a dishonest satrap could abuse the system and withhold tax money for himself, for instance, the king also established a network of undercover officials to watch over the satraps. These officials, who reported only to Darius, were known as "the Eyes and Ears of the King."

The army of Persians under the leadership of Darius was powerful and skilled. At its nucleus was a fighting force of royal bodyguards known as the Immortals: ten thousand warriors who would lay down their lives for their king. Added to that were the hundreds of thousands of soldiers the satraps could provide to the king when requested. Lack of manpower was not an issue in the Persian Empire.

Another of the empire's strengths was its system of rapid communication. Darius I had built a network of military highways known as the Royal Road. It was a system that allowed him to transport troops quick-ly, and to keep in constant contact with all parts of his kingdom using skilled horseback riders as couriers. Under normal circumstances, it might have taken a traveler three or more months to cover the fifteen hundred miles between the cities of Sardis and Susa. The couriers, operating much like America's Pony Express relay riders, could make the trip in a week. With administrative skill and innovations such as the Royal Road, it is no wonder that Darius I's empire was as powerful as it was.

Not Without Weaknesses

But that was the Persian Empire at its peak, two centuries before Alexander. Not all of Darius I's successors were as capable as he. The wealth and power of the empire began to make them unreliable and lazy. Sensing this, many of the satraps took advantage of the situation and built up their own miniature kingdoms with tax money they were supposed to collect for the king. Such corruption was weakening the empire.

Darius III commanded the huge Persian military force.

Signs of this weakness were noticed by the Greeks, reports one historian. "A disgruntled . . . envoy came back from Persia when Philip was a lad, saying that the King had 'plenty of cooks and bakers and confectioners, and hordes of butchers and porters, but men who could look Greek spearmen in the face he had never seen there, and not for the want of trying.'"[52] Because the satraps were often stingy and unwilling to share their armies with the king, the empire had to rely on mercenaries—and the most skilled came from Greece.

By the time Darius III came to the throne in 336 B.C., the empire seemed to be in trouble. Poisonings and plots of murder rocked the royal family. Anxiety and distrust of others was so great that brothers and sisters were marrying one another to maintain the family's control. Darius III himself was the offspring of a brother-sister marriage, and he married his own sister.

An Athenian named Xenophon spent a great deal of time in one of the royal cities of the Persian Empire in the 360s B.C. When he returned to Greece, he listed reasons why he felt there was a "loosening" of the empire which signalled its decline.

> The Persians . . . no longer kept oaths. They extorted money from each other by unjust charges before the king. The king preferred wine to hunting, that essential mark of a bold ruler. The rich nobles refused to send horsemen off their lands to fight the king's wars. They betrayed their horsemanship by using soft-padded saddles. Not even their chariots were properly driven by men whom the owners knew. . . . The court gave in to pleasure.[53]

Alexander was certainly aware of the talk of the Persian Empire's decline. However, he was also aware that even with its weaknesses, the empire was still the most powerful in the world. Darius III, with over one million soldiers at his disposal, would be the most formidable opponent the Macedonian king could imagine.

Without Delay

Just as they had warned him against acting too hastily in squelching the Greek rebellions, Alexander's advisors had words for him before his invasion of Asia. A military attack on Persia might have seemed reckless to them, especially given the difference in size of the Persian- and Macedonian-led armies. Perhaps those closest to Alexander did not realize that their king's impulsiveness was also one of his greatest strengths; he would not be talked out of a springtime invasion.

But the advisors' fears were not simply military. Macedonian nobles worried also about the fate of the kingdom if Alexander were to die in the coming months. He was not married; there were no sons to assume the throne if he were killed in battle. Even his mother agreed that Alexander should attend to these matters before leaving on such a dangerous journey. But nothing convinced her son to postpone his trip.

There was a good reason for Alexander not to delay—money. The Macedonian treasury was empty; in fact, the kingdom was in debt. Philip was responsible for the sad financial state, for although his military conquests brought wealth to the kingdom, he quickly spent the money outfitting his armies for another campaign.

It was a dilemma. On the verge of bankruptcy, Macedon's problems could be solved either by dissolving the army, or by risking everything on the army's success and waiting for the spoils of war to fill the empty coffers. There was no real question which road Alexander would choose. As he remarked later, "I inherited from my father a few gold and silver cups, less than 60 talents in the treasury; and debts of 500 that he owed. When I had borrowed another 800, I set out."[54]

The Royal Ladder

There was a definite chain of command in Asia, from the king and his court to the satraps of various provinces. This was sometimes referred to as the "royal ladder," and is explained by Robin Lane Fox in The Search for Alexander.

"In his province, the satrap himself kept a court that was a local reflection of the central style of the king. In part, this belonged with his own close accountability to the center. The royal secretaries and any royal masters of a garrison were reporters on his actions. Tributes had to be forwarded yearly and wars had to be agreed, in theory, with the king before they were fought. At times, there was a familiar feeling that life in Asia was made impossible by the constraints of the king and his distant officials. There was also a deep-rooted fear in the regions of gossip by dinner companions who had access to the king at his distant court. But the royal ladder lost none of its general allure to men in the provinces. The satrap, too, kept officials on a scale of rations and household payments. He often had his own bodyguard of household troops. . . . Satraps, locally, cast themselves in the image of their king and his court."

Crossing the Hellespont

Alexander left Macedon with thirty thousand infantry soldiers, together with cavalry numbering about five thousand. He left a trusted general, Antipater, to rule in his absence, hoping that the thirteen thousand troops left behind would be enough to keep the wayward Greeks from another rebellion.

Alexander crossed into Asia at a narrow channel known as the Hellespont. Today called the Dardanelles, the channel cuts between the Aegean Sea, on the European side, and the Black Sea of Asia. The crossing was done ferry-style, in galleys. Wanting to be in complete control of his own crossing, Alexander ordered the helmsman of his boat to allow him to steer it himself.

Going from Europe to Asia was a momentous occasion for Alexander. He saw the event as symbolic—just as the Persian general Xerxes had done 150 years before, now he, a Greek leader, was crossing the Hellespont onto foreign soil. And whether out of superstition or just an urge to be dramatic, Alexander wanted the crossing to be as similar to that of Xerxes as possible. Like the Persian, Alexander brought a bull onto the galley, and when he was halfway across the channel, he killed it as a sacrifice to Poseidon, god of the sea. A ceremonial glass of wine was poured into a golden goblet, similar to the one Xerxes had used.

The young king must have been a striking figure, clad in full armor and navigating his ship. Historians know that he was not tall, but was

well proportioned and handsome in a strikingly distinctive way: his brow, the jut of his nose and the set of his lips

Alexander modeled his trip to Asia after the Persian general Xerxes, who had crossed into foreign territory 150 years before.

A woodcut depicts the Trojan Horse. The heroes and legends associated with Troy inspired Alexander throughout his life.

were characteristically "noble," his curling [blond] hair grew in a peak of his forehead, his skin was smooth and slightly florid, and he had a habit of carrying his head and casting his eyes upwards and to the right. . . . His quickness of speech and gait . . . were imitated by his circle, as was his beardlessness. The total effect was of an urgent, impatient boyishness.[55]

When his galley reached the other side of the Hellespont, Alexander took his long spear and flung it into the wet sand of the beach. This land would be taken by force. However, as eager as Alexander was to begin his military campaign, there was one important stop he first had to make.

Echoes from the Past

While his troops made camp and organized themselves, Alexander and his closest advisors went south, to the city of Troy.

Although it was little more than a ruined shell of a place, heaps of rubble and destruction, it was sacred to Alexander. Troy was the site of the Greek and Trojan battles in the war Homer wrote about in *The Iliad* and *The Odyssey*. Troy was the place of heroes and legends that were Alexander's favorite readings as a boy. Says one historian, "Such a moment crackled with echoes from the past for one as steeped as he in Homeric tradition."[56]

If Alexander was mindful of symbols and ritual during his crossing of the Hellespont, his every action at Troy accented his need to be like his heroes. After praying and making a sacrifice at the sanctuary of Athena (a Greek goddess), he exchanged part of his armor for pieces of armor he picked up in the ruins of the city. They would bring him good luck, he told his companions. In fact, he carried many of these relics into battle throughout the Asian campaign; they were, according to historian Robin Lane Fox, "the most traveled antiquities in the ancient world, a lasting witness to his Homeric view of himself."[57]

Plans and Counterplans

Ever mindful of ancient omens and ritual, Alexander laid flowers at the grave of Achilles (pictured, seated) during his trip to Troy.

One of the most obvious attempts at imitating Homer's Trojan War tale occurred at the tomb of Alexander's ancestor, the Greek warrior Achilles. Achilles' best friend Patroclus was buried not far away. Determined to honor Achilles' memory, Alexander laid a garland of flowers at Achilles' grave, and ordered his own best friend, Hephestion, to lay flowers on the grave of Patroclus. From his visit to the ancient city of Troy, Alexander established for himself a link with the past he felt he needed.

As Alexander made his way back to his armies from Troy, the Persian forces were in council less than a two-days' march away. The arrival of the Macedonians was no surprise—the empire's spies had long been aware of Alexander's plans to invade their land. The question now was how best to handle the situation.

Darius was not particularly concerned about Alexander's presence in his country. Writes one historian,

> He was unaware that any danger could come of Macedon, and his opinion was shared by his nobles and the majority of his military staff. What could a nation with so small an army hope to accomplish when faced with the enormous forces of the great Persian Empire?[58]

One military leader who did not share Darius's view, however, was Memnon, a Greek who was the leader of twenty thousand Greek mercenaries fighting for the Persians. He had spent time in Macedon, and knew Alexander's and his well-trained army's capabilities. He proposed to the other generals that the Persian forces retreat, burning and destroying the countryside behind them. Memnon knew that Alexander could not possibly have brought enough supplies from Macedon for his men and horses. By destroying the fields, farms, and orchards, the Persians would be cutting off supplies to their enemies. And without food and other supplies, Memnon said, the Macedonians would be finished in Asia.

But the other generals and satraps loudly disagreed. Destroy their own lands—

some of the most beautiful hunting grounds in the entire empire? Never! It was a cowardly act, they told Memnon scornfully; it was without honor or glory. By fleeing Alexander, the Persians would be admitting that he was a force to be feared.

Battle at the River

Instead, the Persians decided to meet Alexander's forces head on. They would try very hard to kill Alexander early in the battle, for they believed that without their king, the Macedonians would retreat immediately and head back to Greece. The Persians gathered on the east bank of the Granicus River, and as soon as Alexander's spies informed him of the Persian armies' whereabouts, he hurried towards the Granicus, too.

When Alexander's troops arrived at the river, it was late afternoon. Parmenio, one of Alexander's most trusted generals, took one look at the steep banks of the river, swollen to bursting with spring rains, and urged Alexander to reconsider his attack plans. At the very least, Parmenio suggested, they could wait until dawn and mount a surprise attack against the Persians. But Alexander's response should have been predictable by this time. Alexander replied,

All this I know, Parmenio, but I should feel ashamed if after crossing the Hellespont easily this petty stream . . . hinders us from crossing, just as we are. I consider this unworthy either of the prestige of the Macedonians or of my own celerity [speed] in dealing with dangers.[59]

It was pointless to argue with him. Even though Parmenio's fears seemed justified (the slippery riverbanks provided poor footing for advancing troops) Alexander made up his mind. But according to Plutarch,

It seemed the act of a desperate madman, rather than of a prudent commander to charge into a swiftly flowing river, which swept men off their feet and surged about them, and then to advance through a hail of missiles towards a steep bank that was strongly defended by infantry and cavalry.[60]

But Alexander had seen a weakness in the formation of the Persian forces, a weakness that would lead to their defeat that afternoon. The Persian cavalry, waiting on the east side of the river, had been placed in the front line. The Persians sat on their warhorses directly at the edge of the steep embankment. Behind them were Memnon's Greek mercenary foot soldiers. It seemed to Alexander a foolish plan. Why waste powerful, fast horses—valuable in charging the enemy—by placing them in a situation where they had no opportunity to charge? Some modern historians feel that the Persians were more concerned about national pride, fearing that if Greek mercenaries were in the front, it made the Persians seem unimportant or weak.

Whatever their reasons for doing so, the Persians made a grave error, and the brilliant military mind of Alexander seized it as an opportunity. The mounted soldiers on the east bank of the river were blinded by the bright afternoon sun and had no weapons to combat the long sarissas of the advancing Macedonian phalanx. And although they slipped, slid, and occa-

Persians and Macedonians meet head on at the Granicus River. Attempts to drive off the Macedonians proved futile; Alexander's men held their rank and emerged victorious.

sionally lost footing as they crossed the Granicus, Alexander's hoplites held their ranks. Confused and frightened by the long, sharp spears thrust in their faces, the Persian cavalry retreated.

Behind the cavalry, the Greek mercenaries fought on for a while, but soon realized that they, too, were doomed. They begged Alexander for mercy, but he refused, wanting to make an example of them for their traitorous behavior. According to Arrian, Alexander shouted to his men that they should let "not one get away except by escaping notice among the dead."[61] Alexander's men followed his orders, slaughtering the helpless Greeks by the thousands.

The Spoils of War

The Greek mercenaries were not the only losses on the Persian side. Darius, although he himself was not present at the battle, lost a son-in-law and a brother-in-law. Several satraps and other nobles were killed, leaving their provinces in the hands of inexperienced deputies.

Figures and statistics of the battle—how many died and how many were taken prisoner—are difficult to interpret. Many ancient historians were writing to glorify the Greeks, or Alexander in particular, so his armies' losses in battle are minimized, while the Persian figures are exaggerated. In this battle, the Persian forces are said to have had twelve thousand killed, while Alexander's army only suffered ninety casualties. No matter how exaggerated the numbers, historians agree that this battle was a clear victory for Alexander.

He took twenty thousand prisoners and sent them back to Macedon to do hard labor. He also sent a shipment of three hundred shields taken from dead Persian soldiers to Athens. He enclosed a note to show that he was still anxious to keep the support of the Athenians: "Alexander, son of Philip, and all the Greeks, except Sparta, won these spoils of war from the barbarians who dwell in Asia."[62] He did not forget his mother, either; he sent crates of plundered goods home to Olympias.

After the battle, Alexander endeared himself to the backbone of the campaign—the foot soldiers who risked their lives for him. Time and again, he showed his men how much he needed and valued them. He appreciated their support, and they knew it. Families of men who died in battle were granted immunity from taxes and excused from all their debts. He personally took charge of the burial of his soldiers. The wounded were given special attention, too. As Arrian relates, "He took great care of the wounded, visiting each man himself, examining their wounds, asking how they were received and allowing them to recount and boast of their exploits."[63]

The men under Alexander's command responded to his interest with fierce devotion. They would lay down their lives for him, and they knew he would do the same for them. They would have ample opportunity to prove their devotion. They had all survived the first battle in Asia. There would be many more.

5 Storming Across Asia

Alexander's overwhelming victory over the Persian troops at Granicus must have excited his troops. Realizing that they had taken up arms against the largest empire in the world and emerged victorious probably made the Macedonian and Greek forces eager to fight again. But no more fighting was to occur for a while—it was completely unnecessary.

Like Ripe Fruit

The Persian forces had retreated quickly, needing to regroup and rethink their strategy against Alexander. And all the cities near Alexander's troops were Greek—the very cities he had set out to liberate. Although they were ruled by Persian officials, the citizens were Greek, and were thrilled at Alexander's arrival. Cities such as Zeleia, Sardis, Ephesus, and Lampsacus sent messengers to meet the Macedonian troops, and the Persian officials, realizing that to fight would be pointless, surrendered quickly. The Greek cities along the coast of Asia Minor, writes Mary Renault, "fell to him like ripe fruit."[64]

Alexander was kind to these cities. Arrian reports that "he ordered the oligarchies [government by a few] everywhere to be overthrown and democracies to be established; he restored its own laws to each city and remitted the tribute they used to pay to [the Persians]."[65] However, he did expect the citizens of the liberated cities to pay tribute to him and his army to finance the next months of their campaign, but they did this willingly.

Alexander also made certain that the people were free to keep the laws and customs to which they were accustomed. Like the first Darius, Alexander needed the support of the people whose lands he conquered. He did not have enough troops to leave behind a military regime in every city and territory. It made no sense to him to take more than he needed from his subjects. When asked why, for instance, he did not levy higher taxes on the people he conquered, Alexander once said, "I hate the gardener who cuts to the root the vegetables of which he ought to cull the leaves."[66]

The Eagle on the Mast

Alexander and his forces headed south down the coast toward the key port city of Miletus. The people of that city were ready to surrender to Alexander as the other cities had done. But just before they sent

A view of the coast of Asia Minor. According to Mary Renault, the Greek cities along this coast fell to Alexander "like ripe fruit."

their messengers to ask for peace, they heard that a large fleet of Persian ships was on its way to their harbor. Aid from the Persians meant that they did not have to surrender after all.

Alexander acted quickly. He knew that a huge, four-hundred-ship Persian fleet was bringing thousands of troops to Miletus to fight his army, but he also knew that those troops would be useless until they landed. His mission, then, was to keep the Persian fleet out of the harbor, so the men and supplies could not be unloaded.

He had brought with him a fleet of 160 ships—most were not Macedonian ships, but rather were supplied by the League of Corinth. He ordered them into the harbor, setting a blockade for the 400-ship fleet of the Persians. Although Memnon and the Persians waited, prowling back and forth in front of the harbor, the Greek fleet would not move. There was to be no port of call for the Persian fleet.

Without the assistance of the additional soldiers on the ships, Miletus could not fight for long against Alexander's army. The mighty catapults and other siege engines of the Macedonian troops crashed through Miletus's outer walls, and Alexander's men overran the city.

During this time, Alexander's general Parmenio came to him with exciting news of an omen. The general had been looking at one of the league's ships, partially aground in the harbor at Miletus, when he noticed an eagle perched on the mast. He told Alexander that because the eagle was looking out to sea, it indicated that victory for the Macedonians lay in a sea attack. Parmenio urged his king to push out from the harbor and fight the Persian fleet. Besides, he argued, what could they lose? The Persian fleet, which was more than twice the size of the league's, was obviously superior. Any damage the league's ships could inflict would only help Alexander's forces, and if the league were beaten, no one would be surprised.

But Alexander disagreed. He felt it would be foolish to waste his sailors and their ships in a useless battle with the Persians. As Arrian writes,

[Alexander] would not risk sacrificing the experience and daring of the Macedonians to the [Persians] on so uncertain an element; if they lost the engagement, it would be a serious blow to their initial prestige in the war, especially with the Greeks also ready to blaze into revolt at the news of a naval defeat.[67]

Neutralizing Persian Sea Power

He also thought that Parmenio had misread the omen. The eagle was definitely on the mast, but since the boat was on the beach, Alexander felt that the omen really meant that he would beat the Persian fleet not at sea, but on land. Although ancient historians do not relate Parmenio's reaction, it must have surprised him to be more impulsive than Alexander. But what was Alexander thinking? How could the Macedonian army defeat the most powerful fleet in the ancient world—on land?

The victory at Miletus had given Alexander an idea that could solve a difficult problem. Throughout his planning for the Persian invasion, Alexander had been troubled by the superiority of the Asian fleet. Until now, he had not considered that sea power could be changed into a liability.

In those days, a navy was not as self-reliant as a modern navy. The crew, the

large number of rowers needed to propel the ships, and the thousands of troops being transported required an unbelievably large amount of fresh water and supplies. All ancient warships sailed with supporting land troops, who provided the ships with supplies.

Alexander had observed that the four hundred Persian ships that came to Miletus did so without any land support. When they could not land and had no ground troops to help them gather supplies, the ships had no alternative but to leave. If his armies controlled every city along the coast, Alexander reasoned, he could neutralize Darius's sea power, for the ships would be unable to land!

When autumn arrived, Alexander and his men did just that. Following a path around the coast of Asia Minor, the Macedonian army captured cities along the sea, removing the threat of the mighty Persian fleet. As naval battles were unnecessary, he saw that his own fleet of league ships was not needed for the time being. Alexander kept about twenty of the ships to be used for supplies and transport of the war machines, and sent the rest back to Greece.

Undoing the Knot

Winter was fast approaching, and Alexander was aware that his men had been working hard. Many soldiers had married shortly before setting out from Macedon, and to these he granted leave for the winter months. Married soldiers could go home and spend time with their wives until spring. The remaining troops would continue with Alexander through the coastal cities of Asia Minor. As usual, Alexander's

Ancient War Technology

One of the advantages Alexander had over many of his enemies was his mastery of various siege machines. These were brought on nearly every campaign, for they were valuable tools, as historian Frank Lipsius points out in his book Alexander the Great.

"Then, as now, warfare was a spur to technology. At that time, siege-machines were capable of flinging a fifty-pound stone ball five hundred feet. Alexander's father Philip had been the first to use them in eastern Greece and while the torsion pressure of the machines was no greater than a woman's twisted braid, they transformed the art of war. Not only did they allow attacks on an enemy in the winter (when city life retreated behind its protective wall) but they also marked a significant advance in an age of primitive technology. Bolts and screws were unknown. There was no rope, twine, springs, or adhesive materials. No lubricants. Soda and oil were used to clean cloth, but there was no soap. Pulleys and gears were little understood."

Siege machines were invaluable in Alexander's campaigns against the Persians.

care and concern for his men paid off in their loyalty. As Arrian writes, "Alexander gained as much popularity by this act among the Macedonians as by any other."[68]

By spring, expecting his troops fresh from their leave in Macedonia, Alexander

felt he had controlled the coast and decided to travel inland, to Gordium. Gordium, in what today is Turkey, was the site of an ancient, mysterious relic known as the Gordian knot. This was really a wagon—a two-wheeled, wooden wagon that legend

In Gordium, the impatient and clever Alexander undid the legendary Gordian knot. Thus, according to legend, Alexander would become lord of all Asia.

possible to undo because no ends were visible; there was nothing to work at or unravel. Knowing what historians say about Alexander's nature, it is not difficult to imagine his obsession with solving the puzzle.

Two versions exist of the story of Alexander's adventure with the Gordian knot. One says that he did what no one had thought of before; he slid the yoke out of the knot, revealing the hidden ends that could then be untied.

The other version tells of an impatient Alexander who grew frustrated with puzzling over the impossible knot. He "solved" the knot by drawing his sword and cutting it. In modern times, the phrase "cutting the Gordian knot" means to get through to the heart of a problem by tackling it forcefully, exactly as King Alexander is said to have done in Gordium.

No one knows whether either version is true. Arrian writes,

> I cannot say with confidence what Alexander actually did about this knot, but he . . . certainly left the wagon with the impression that the oracle had been fulfilled, and in fact that night there was thunder and lightning, a further sign from heaven . . . so Alexander in thanksgiving offered sacrifice next day to whatever gods had shown the signs and the way to undo the knot.[69]

Death Averted

said once belonged to the famed King Midas, who had received the gift of the golden touch.

The yoke was fastened to the wagon by a complicated knot made of thongs of cornel bark. According to a Gordian legend, whoever undid the knot would become the lord of all Asia. The knot seemed im-

Darius III, often called the Great King in ancient literature, was forced to rethink his impression of Alexander. The Macedonians' success in Asia Minor had surprised him, and as the summer of 333 B.C. arrived, Darius busied himself collecting an army from the various satraps. Alexander, meanwhile, was pleased that his army was back to full strength after the winter leave of many of his regulars. Before the two armies met, however, Alexander had a narrow escape which had nothing at all to do with battle.

Alexander and his army were making a particularly difficult march through the Taurus Mountains in the southern part of Asia Minor. The march had left the king hot, sweaty, and exhausted. When they came to the cold, melted-snow waters of the Cydnus River, Alexander stripped and dove in. The shock of the icy water almost paralyzed him; his aides dragged him out, grayish-white and cramped.

For days he lay with a high fever. The army physicians were afraid to try their medicine on him, says Plutarch, "for they all believed that his condition was so dangerous that medicine was powerless to help him, and dreaded the accusations that would be brought against them by the Macedonians in the event of their failure."[70]

The Macedonian troops were beside themselves with anxiety and fright, believing that their beloved captain would soon die. "As tidings of their leader's danger spread through the camp," writes one historian, "the whole army, officers, and soldiers, were thrown into the greatest consternation and grief."[71]

One physician, however, was not afraid. Philip, a friend of Alexander's since boyhood, was willing to treat the king. He prepared a strong drink that he believed would cleanse Alexander's body of the fever that was making him so ill. Before the king drank the medicine, he handed a letter to Philip that had been delivered that day. It was a warning from Parmenio, saying that Darius had bribed Philip to poison the Macedonian.

Before Philip could finish the letter and protest his innocence, Alexander drank the medicine. The cure worked, and Alexander recovered. The army re-

Alexander often demonstrated fierce loyalty to his men. In one instance, a feverish Alexander drank medicine given to him by a physician friend, despite a note accusing the physician of intent to poison him.

joiced at the news, happy that their adventure would continue. Just as important, however, was the image Alexander showed to his entire army. "He was resolute in refusing to suspect his friends," writes Arrian, "and steadfast in the face of death."[72] This was the kind of king he had learned to be during his philosophy and history lessons with Aristotle—a strong, self-assured leader, rather than the hostile, always-suspicious ruler who commonly appeared throughout history. This was the kind of man who would lead the Macedonian and Greek armies to glory.

From Liberator to Conqueror

For two months Alexander rested, regaining his strength. During this time, Darius's armies grew to an estimated 600,000 men, according to Plutarch, although other historians claim the total was between 300,000 and 400,000. But if the size of the Persian army was even close to these estimates, it far outnumbered Alexander's army. Many of his soldiers had been hit by a fever that summer, and even including his cavalry and the soldiers he had added from friendly cities of Asia, his forces numbered only about 30,000.

As he recruited more men for his army, Darius became more alarmed. Alexander was no longer merely liberating Greek cities in Asia Minor. No longer could his actions be called revenge against the Persian Empire. He had crossed the Taurus Mountains, and was heading south. There were no more Greek cities to liberate. He had crossed the line from "liberator" to "conqueror." Darius knew

that unless he moved quickly against the invader, his empire was in jeopardy.

For weeks, the two armies moved toward one another. Alexander headed south from the home bases he had established in conquered territories; Darius moved west from Babylonia. Both armies moved quickly, trying to be the first to establish a position for battle that would give their army superiority. Alexander was confident that Darius would take a position on the wide plains, giving his huge cavalry room to charge the Macedonian troops.

Then Darius made a move that seemed to be a stroke of genius. Instead of continuing his westerly march, he followed a military path unknown to the Macedonians and swung his huge army north, into territory that Alexander had just marched through. Near Issus, at the border of present-day Syria and Turkey, Darius came to a field hospital set up by Alexander.

Hundreds of sick and wounded men were recuperating there, but Darius showed an ugly, brutal side to his nature. Many of the patients were killed, while others were lined up by the Persians, who chopped off their hands. Making the torture even more painful, Darius ordered his army to burn the bloody stumps with hot tar. The Great King took the victims, screaming in agony, to tour his massive Persian army. He then turned the men loose, instructing them to hurry and tell Alexander what they had just seen.

Fighting Fear

Alexander's troops were terrified. The intelligence reports, in addition to the frightened accounts of the torture victims from

Eating with Alexander

Plutarch, in his book The Age of Alexander, *describes how even an activity as common as eating dinner was very elaborate if one was in the company of Alexander.*

"His custom was not to begin supper until late, as it was growing dark. He took it reclining on a couch, and he was wonderfully attentive and observant in ensuring that his table was well provided, his guests equally served, and none of them neglected. He sat long over his wine . . . because of his fondness for conversation. . . . As for delicacies, Alexander was so restrained in his appetite that often when the rarest fruits or fish were brought to him from the sea coast, he would distribute them so generously among his companions that there would be nothing left for himself. His evening meal, however, was always a magnificent affair, and as his successes multiplied, so did his expenditure on hospitality."

Issus, made it clear that Darius had completely fooled the Macedonian army. The Persians had cut across the rear of Alexander's forces, severing them from their communication links, supply stations, home base, and a safe path of retreat.

Realizing that panic and fear could do more damage among his troops than even Darius's forces, Alexander spoke to his men. In his most persuasive voice, he told them the story of another Greek force many years ago. Like the Macedonian army, it, too, was cut off from its home base without the support of additional troops. He reminded his men how that long-ago army had used their inner strength and determination to fight their way out of that danger.

According to ancient historians, Alexander could sense that his men were beginning to relax a little. He went on, says Arrian, and told them "of anything else which at such a time, before dangers, a brave general would naturally tell brave men by way of encouragement."[73] And when he had convinced them that they, too, could fight their way out of this situation, they responded with confidence. Explains Arrian, "They crowded around and clasped their king's hand, and with cries of encouragement urged him to lead them on at once."[74]

The Great King at Last

Alexander's army made a quick about-face, so that they could meet Darius head-on. The two forces met up near Issus, on a narrow coastal plain between the mountains and the sea. Alexander had been impressed with Darius's strategy in cutting off the Macedonian army from their

Darius sits high in his chariot as Alexander thunders toward him at the battle of Issus. Soon after, Darius turned and fled for his life.

home base. But the Great King's plan had a serious flaw, which was evident as the armies waited for the signal to begin the battle.

Darius, commanding a force of hundreds of thousands, was bottled up in a very narrow space. Perched on a high river bank, as they had been at Granicus, the Persian soldiers were in a defensive, rather than an offensive stance.

Alexander, mounted on his favorite horse Bucephalas, moved up and down the lines of his troops, telling his officers how brave and cunning they were, lifting their spirits as he had done the night before. Historians say that Alexander quite probably knew the names of several thousand men in his army, a feat which reaped rich rewards in times like these. Morale and spirit were invaluable, and the Macedonians were eager to perform bravely for their king.

Alexander was also excited, for this was the first time he had come face-to-face with the king of Persia. Darius was almost a giant by the standards of those days—almost six-and-a-half feet tall. His long, silver hair and flowing, purple robes must have made him a striking figure on the battlefield. At fifty, Darius was more than twice the age of the Macedonian king.

But the younger man gave the signal to attack first, and the Macedonian army attacked with a viciousness the Persians had never seen before. The bristling sarissas of Alexander's phalanx drove the Persians back, collapsing their infantry line. Larger numbers did not give the Persians an advantage, for they were cramped into such a small area they could not maneuver as they would have liked. Darius tried to compensate for his mistake by splitting his army into smaller forces.

But it was no use. The Persians fought bravely, but finally their line crumpled. As their cavalry wheeled in retreat, they trampled thousands of infantry who were standing behind them. In the confusion, Arrian reports, Alexander's troops "fell on them with vigor, and there was as much slaughter in the cavalry-flight as in the infantry."[75]

Darius, who had watched his troops being driven back further and further, fled in panic. He was in a chariot, which on level ground was a quick way to travel. But, says Arrian:

> When he came to gullies and other difficult patches, he left his chariot there, threw away his shield and mantle [cloak], left even his bow in the chariot, and fled on horseback; only night, speedily falling, saved him from becoming Alexander's captive.[76]

"This Is What It Is to Be King"

Though he pursued Darius, Alexander was unable to catch him. He was able, however, to capture the Great King's camp, and when Alexander and his officers saw how Darius lived on military campaigns, they were flabbergasted. He traveled with a full staff of nobles, servants, dancers, singers, and other entertainers.

His tents were like a miniature palace—the first was a luxurious bathroom, with basins, pitchers, and baths carved and decorated in gold. According to Plutarch, Alexander passed from that tent

> into a spacious and lofty tent [and] observed the magnificence of the dining couches, the tables, and the banquet which had been set out for him. He turned to his companions and remarked, "So this, it seems, is what it is to be a king."[77]

Darius flees for his life at the battle of Issus. According to Arrian, "Only night, speedily falling, saved him from becoming Alexander's captive."

Alexander with Darius's wife, mother, and daughters. In those days, women were considered spoils of war, yet Alexander treated the women with kindness and respect.

While eating that evening, Alexander was puzzled to hear loud wailing and crying coming from another section of the captured camp. He was informed that Darius's wife, mother, and two young daughters were at the camp. They had seen Darius's bow, chariot, and robe and thought he was dead. Alexander was struck silent for some time, writes Plutarch, "for he was evidently more affected by the women's grief than by his own triumph."[78]

He sent his aides to their tent to inform the women that Darius was not dead; he had fled for his life from Alexander and his troops. Alexander, together with his close friend Hephestion, visited the tent himself later that evening. When the two men walked in, Sisygambis, Darius's mother, fell on her knees in front of Hephestion. Hephestion was taller than Alexander, and since the Asians equated height with royalty, she believed him to be king.

When she realized her error, the woman fell back, frightened that she had insulted Alexander. But according to historians, Alexander stepped forward and with a smile, raised her up. "Never mind, Mother," he said, "you made no mistake—he, too, is Alexander."[79] Whether he was simply making a joke to put her at ease, or he meant that he and Hephestion were so close that they were almost the same person is unclear.

What *was* clear, however, was that Alexander was bucking tradition in his treatment of Darius's family. Women in those days were considered no more than property; when captured they were divided up among the victors as any other spoils of war. Darius's wife, Statiera, was considered the most beautiful woman in Asia, and few would have protested had Alexander demanded that she become his mistress.

Instead, he was gentle and compassionate. He assured the women that they and the two girls would be protected and cared for in the style to which they were accustomed. They would retain their status of royalty. As Plutarch reports, Alexander assured them "that they should never hear, suspect, nor have cause to fear anything which could disgrace them."[80]

He was true to his word. Treating them as his own adopted family, Alexander allowed them to travel with him during the military campaign. With Sisygambis, Darius's mother, he enjoyed a warm friendship. She was so fond of the young king, in fact, that years later when she learned of his death, she turned her face to the wall and refused to speak or eat. She died of starvation within five days.

Some historians, however, feel that Alexander's reluctance to claim Darius's wife for himself was not merely compassionate. He was, they say, disinterested in sex. Plutarch writes that Alexander felt it was "more worthy of a king to subdue his own passions than to conquer his enemies."[81] He associated with no women, although he was frequently encouraged by his aides to take a Persian mistress. Historians report that he refused, saying "These Persian women are an irritation to our eyes." Says Plutarch, "He was determined to make such a show of his chastity and self-control as to eclipse the beauty of their appearance, so he passed by them as if they had been so many lifeless images cast out of stone."[82]

Other Spoils of War

For Alexander, the rewards of victory were confined to objects instead of people. The victory at Issus was a profitable one. Golden goblets, ornaments, fine rugs, and jewelry were among the spoils of war shared with officers and friends.

For himself, he kept only a beautiful jeweled casket that had belonged to Darius. He used it as the traveling box for his treasured copy of *The Iliad*, which Aristotle had given him.

Alexander sent treasures back home, too. His mother received some of the most lavish jewelry and ornaments. He also sent many treasures and full suits of armor back to Athens. Interestingly, the Athenians were still unwilling to praise the Macedonian: historian Agnes Savill writes that "his gifts were coldly received."[83]

An Offer Rejected

In exile, Darius wrote to Alexander, offering to stop the war if Alexander would return his family to him. But Alexander did not want an alliance with Darius. He wrote to Darius,

> I am, by gift of the gods, in possession of your land. . . . Come to me then, and ask for your mother, wife, and children. . . . But for the future, whenever you send to me, send to me as the king of Asia . . . and if you dispute my right to the kingdom, stay and fight another battle for it; but do not run away. For whatever you do, I intend to march against you.[84]

Peace was not an option for Alexander. He did not welcome it, for he was just beginning what he had perhaps always intended to do—conquer the entire Persian Empire. The war would continue.

6 From Tyre to Egypt

Not long after his victory at Issus, Alexander announced to his staff that he intended to march southwest, into Egypt. Besides wanting to conquer this large desert kingdom, Alexander wanted to establish bases there before he launched east into the center of Asia.

In order for his plan to work, it was important to neutralize the Persian navy. The Persian ships controlled the southeast part of the Mediterranean Sea and could make trouble for the invading Macedonians. Just as he had done in Asia Minor, Alexander proposed to fight the enemy's navy by controlling its harbors.

The city of Tyre, located in present-day Lebanon, was the Persians' most powerful naval base. Tyre was actually two cities: one on land and another half a mile from shore on an island. The island, the site of the huge naval base, would be the problem. Around the rocky island the Tyrians had built a 150-foot-high wall to protect their city. The forty thousand citizens of Tyre received their supplies by sea, via two harbors on the island.

Tyre had a history of being impenetrable. Many had tried to invade over the centuries, most notably the famous King Nebuchadnezzar of Babylonia, who two centuries before had besieged the island for thirteen years. None had been success-

ful. To defeat the Tyrians, Alexander knew he had to bring down the walls. But how? The machines on which he normally relied to knock down city walls—catapults and battering rams—would be of no use half a mile from their target.

As on other military campaigns, Alexander had brought with him some non-military people, such as botanists and zoologists, to study and record the new things found on the campaign. Among these experts was an engineer named Diades. To his credit, Alexander understood the limits of his army, and was not too proud to turn to others for help. The conquest of Tyre, he knew, could not be accomplished with soldiers' courage and bravery alone. For the Macedonians, the problem was not a military one, but an engineering one.

Building a Mole

The solution, according to the engineers, was to build a mole, a small, raised road that would lead from the shore out to the island of Tyre. Once the mole was constructed, the catapults and other machinery could be wheeled to within striking range, and the siege of Tyre could begin.

The idea seemed a good one, and the Macedonians set to work. The first order of business was to assemble all the material needed for the mole. Alexander and his troops had little trouble defeating the on-shore city of Tyre, which gave up without much of a struggle. After it was conquered, it was leveled, and the stone and rock were hauled to the water's edge to begin building the road. The endless inland forests provided the men with lumber, and there was plenty of cementlike mud along the shore to hold it all together.

As the mole inched farther and farther out from shore, the Macedonians built high wooden towers that moved along with it. There were large missile engines in the towers, which flung rocks and spears at the walls of the city. Although the Tyrians fought back, shooting flaming arrows, those inside the towers were protected by large blankets of rawhide. It seemed as though the taking of Tyre would be easier than Alexander had been led to believe.

The project was made easier by the willingness of Alexander's men to be construction workers rather than soldiers for a while. According to Arrian, the enthusiasm of the king himself had created the strong morale. "The Macedonians were very eager for the work, like Alexander; he was present directing each step himself, inspired the men with his words, and encouraged their exertions by gifts to those who did work of exceptional merit."[85]

Not Enough

During this time, a letter arrived for Alexander. It was from Darius and contained a proposal for peace. The Great

Amidst a deluge of arrows, Alexander directs the construction of the mole that would lead the Macedonians to Tyre.

King was anxious to get his family back, and offered Alexander 10,000 talents (about $300,000) as ransom. In addition, Darius said he would give all of his empire west of the Euphrates River, as well as his oldest daughter in marriage, to the Macedonian king.

Alexander's aides were ecstatic. This was far more than they had ever hoped for—it was almost unbelievable! Alexander's general Parmenio congratulated the king on his "victory" and advised him to take up Darius on his offer. There would

The Macedonians used a variety of battering rams and catapults to crumble the thick walls of Tyre. Despite valiant efforts to rout the advancing Macedonians, the Tyrians were no match for Alexander.

be no further loss of life, and Alexander would surely enjoy a most remarkable conquest. Parmenio added that if he were Alexander, that was what he would do. "So would I, if I were Parmenio," replied the king.[86]

Alexander wrote back to Darius, telling him that he had no need of money, and that if he wanted to marry his daughter, he would simply do so. He did not need Darius's permission or blessing. Finally, he informed Darius that he did not intend to settle for part of a kingdom—specifically the area west of the Euphrates River. Writes one historian:

> He had crossed too many seas in his military expeditions to feel any concern about the rivers that he might find in his way; and that he should continue to pursue Darius wherever he might retreat in search of safety and protection, and he had no fear

but that he should find and conquer him at last.[87]

Alexander was less interested in Darius than in the trouble his men were having in Tyre. The easy engineering solution was turning into a nightmare.

The Tyrians' Revenge

Work on the mole was slow, and the Tyrians took advantage of the laborers' difficulty. As the road progressed farther out to sea, the Tyrians' opposition to the construction became more aggressive. From the thick city walls, archers sent hundreds of arrows at workers. Ships, too, were sent out to sabotage the building efforts. In one instance, the Tyrians loaded a ship with pitch sulfur, wood shavings, and other combustible material and set it ablaze near the mole with fire arrows. It was a successful move—both Alexander's wooden towers burned down.

One of the Tyrians' most effective weapons was sand, heated in large cauldrons until it was red hot. They shot it from catapults at the Macedonian workers. According to the historian Diodorus, "It sifted down under their corselets and their clothes, searing the flesh with intense heat. . . . They screamed entreaties like men under torture, and none could help them, but with the excruciating pain they went mad and died."[88]

Butchery at Tyre

Alexander knew that the mole would not be completed unless his workers were protected from the Tyrian ships, which were buzzing around them like angry wasps. His own navy had returned to Macedon and Greece long before, on his command. Even if he were to send a message back to Macedon for the ships to return, he could not rely on their making the voyage to Tyre in time to save his troops.

Help came first from the Phoenicians, who contributed 80 warships to Alexander's cause. Soon afterward, 120 ships from other allies arrived. Their sailors had heard of Alexander's reputation as a brave, ingenious leader and decided they would be better off on the Macedonian-Greek side of any war. With support from these warships, Alexander and his men were able to finish the small road.

If Alexander expected a quick victory upon completion of the mole, he was mistaken. To his frustration, his battering rams and catapults had only limited success in battering down the city walls. The Tyrians had strengthened their walls so well that the huge siege machines of the Macedonians were, says one historian, "no more effective than men's fists would have been."[89]

Alexander then chained many ships together and built a large platform over them. The ships could be rowed right up

Phoenician mariners allied themselves with Alexander and helped him complete the road to Tyre.

The Slaughter at Tyre

In his book History of Alexander the Great, *Jacob Abbott describes the moment that Alexander's army was finally able to break through the heavy walls of Tyre and assault the city.*

"The ships advanced to the proposed place for landing. The bridges were let down. The men crowded over them to the foot of the wall. They clambered up through the breach to the battlements above, although the Tyrians thronged the passage and made the most desperate resistance. Hundreds were killed by darts and arrows, and falling stones, and their bodies tumbled into the sea. The others, paying no attention to their falling comrades, and drowning the horrid screams of the crushed and the dying with their own frantic shouts of rage and fury, pressed on up the broken wall till they reached the battlements above. The vast throng then rolled along upon the top of the wall till they came to stairways and slopes by which they could descend into the city, and pouring down through all these avenues, they spread over the streets, and satiated the hatred and the rage, which had been gathering strength all that came in their way. Thus the city was stormed."

to the walls of Tyre, and his soldiers could stand on the platform and fight. But the Tyrians threw heavy rocks into the water near shore, preventing the ships from coming too close. Those that managed to come within striking range faced other dangers—the Tyrians dangled large fishing nets from the walls and snared some of the Macedonian soldiers. These unfortunate men were tortured and killed on top of the city walls, in full view of their horrified comrades.

The Tyrians' savagery backfired, however. When the Macedonians finally mounted a successful attack, storming three sides of the island with ships and siege engines, a large segment of one wall collapsed. Using his finest battalion of hoplites, Alexander was able to gain entrance to the city. As the terrified Tyrians watched the Macedonians pour over the wall, they fled to the center of the city. But there was no mercy that day; on orders from their king, the Macedonians repaid in full the cruelty of the Tyrians. For seven long months the Macedonians had labored and watched their friends die at the hands of the Tyrians. Now it was their turn.

As one historian writes:

When the last organized resistance was broken, Alexander's veterans ranged through the city on a ferocious manhunt, all restraint abandoned, hysterical and half-crazy after the long rigors of that dreadful siege, mere butchers now, striking and trampling and tearing limb from limb until Tyre became a bloody, reeking abattoir [slaughterhouse].[90]

Many Tyrians tried to escape the butchery by locking themselves in their homes and committing suicide. Most, however, were slaughtered by Alexander's men as they ran screaming from their attackers. Seven thousand Tyrians were murdered that day. Alexander ordered that two thousand others, mostly young men of military age, be taken down to the shore and crucified. The rest of the Tyrians (mostly women and children) were sold into slavery.

It was the summer of 332 B.C. With Tyre a bloodsoaked shambles, Alexander knew that the eastern part of the Mediterranean Sea was now firmly in his control. He turned away from Tyre and headed toward Egypt.

Omens and Walls

As Alexander and his army marched south, they faced no real problems. Many of the people they met had heard the tale of Tyre and did not wish to fight such vicious men. Alexander did not encounter any opposition until he and his men had traveled 150 miles.

The city was Gaza. Alexander had hoped that the satrap, Batis, would give up without a fight, based on the ever-spreading reputation of the Macedonians. But Batis had no intention of giving up his city; just as the governor of Tyre had thought his city impenetrable, Batis was confident that Alexander could not overtake his city. One look at Gaza would explain his confidence—it was located on top of a steep hill, and its walls were monstrously high.

Alexander must have been tempted to leave Gaza and resume his journey to Egypt. After all, the city was not on the coast and had little to do with Alexander's control of the Mediterranean. But to leave a hostile city behind him, especially one as large as Gaza, would have been foolish. Eventually, he knew, the Gazans would threaten his empire. Alexander's men would therefore take up arms against an enemy that seemed impossible to conquer.

As in Tyre, the Macedonians' siege engines were useless. They could not reach the high walls of Gaza, for the hillside was far too steep. Again, Alexander turned to his engineers. And again, his men would have to be laborers before they could be soldiers.

This time, instead of building a road, the Macedonians built steep ramps on which their siege engines could be moved to the walls of Gaza. The construction did not take as long as the mole at Tyre, but the work was hot and difficult. The Gazans slowed the work considerably by bombarding the workers with arrows, spears, and rocks.

While Alexander was inspecting the construction of the ramps, a bird of prey flying overhead dropped a stone on him. Luckily, he was wearing a helmet and was not seriously hurt. But the fact that a bird had caused the one-in-a-million injury worried Alexander. Surely, this did not bode well for his upcoming battle with the Gazans? He consulted the royal soothsay-

After the conquest of Tyre, the Macedonians marched south to Gaza. Finding opposition there, Alexander showed no mercy in taking the city.

At last the city walls crumbled. The Macedonians had helped their cause by digging in the soft sand under the walls, making them unsteady in places. And the Gazans, like the Tyrians, were shown no mercy by Alexander and his troops. One historian reports that "[Alexander's] blood was up and his troops were ready for the slaughter, their temper soured by the weeks of hardships preparing for the assault. . . . The predictable massacre followed, as the fighting men of Gaza were exterminated."[91] With no opposition left in his wake, Alexander moved south from Gaza, toward Egypt.

Alexander and his troops in Egypt. Dissatisfied with Persian rule, Egyptians welcomed Alexander as a liberator.

ers. Their answers were a warning: there would be victory for Alexander at Gaza, but also danger. He should be very careful about his personal safety.

The soothsayers' warning conflicted with Alexander's usual fighting style of leading his army. In the end, though, Alexander adhered to his devout belief in omens and signs. He did what his soothsayers suggested and tried to keep out of range. Even so, he was seriously wounded by a shot from a Gazan catapult. Historians say that Alexander continued to direct his men in battle, although blood poured from the wound under his armor.

Incense for Leonidas

After his army laid siege to the important city of Gaza, Alexander sent many gifts home to his mother and friends. Another person he remembered with a gift was his old tutor, Leonidas, as Plutarch relates in his The Age of Alexander.

"[Alexander] also remembered his tutor Leonidas and presented him with five hundred talents' weight of frankincense and one hundred of myrrh: this was in remembrance of the hopes with which his teacher had inspired him in his boyhood. It seems that one day when Alexander was sacrificing and was throwing incense onto the altar by the handful, Leonidas remarked to him, 'Alexander, when you have conquered the countries that produce these spices, you can make as extravagant sacrifices as you like: till then, don't waste it!' On this occasion Alexander wrote to him, 'I have sent you plenty of myrrh and frankincense, so that you need not be stingy towards the gods any longer.'"

With Open Arms

In Memphis, Alexander sacrifices to Apis, an important Egyptian god.

The Egyptian satraps were well aware of Alexander's success. They yielded to him without hesitation—and not just because of his brutal reputation. Unlike some of the places Alexander had visited, Egypt was very dissatisfied with Persian rule. The Egyptian people had a long, proud history; their own empire was once the most powerful on earth. Since the fifth century B.C., they had been reduced to a tip of the Persian Empire, and they resented it. To them, Alexander represented a change for the better.

The Macedonian king was accepted with open arms and was immediately given the title of pharaoh. He sailed down the east bank of the mighty Nile River to Memphis to see the palace and throne which were now rightfully his. In Memphis

Construction Rather than Destruction

As Jacob Abbott comments in his book History of Alexander the Great, *Alexander's career was almost entirely spent on destroying cities. But during his time in Egypt, he was able to plan the building of one, the city he named Alexandria.*

"In building the city of Alexandria, Alexander laid aside, for a time, his natural and proper character, and assumed a mode of action in strong contrast with the ordinary course of his life. He was, throughout most of his career, a destroyer. He roamed over the world to interrupt commerce, to break in upon and disturb the peaceful pursuits of industry, to batter down city walls, and burn dwellings, and kill men. This is the true vocation of a hero and a conqueror; but at the mouth of the Nile Alexander laid aside this character. He turned his energies to the planning means to do good. He constructed a port; he built warehouses, he provided accommodations and protections for merchants and artisans. . . . How much better would it have been for the happiness of mankind, as well as for his own true fame and glory, if doing good had been the rule of his life instead of the exception."

Alexander maps out plans for the city of Alexandria, which would become a center of learning and culture.

he pleased the Egyptian priests by sacrificing to Apis, one of their important gods.

Soon afterwards, Alexander sailed back along the western branch of the Nile. He came to a lovely spot near the Mediterranean coast, where two harbors nestled between a lagoon and the sea. It would be, he suggested, an ideal site for a city. It would have a large forum, a university, a library, and temples honoring both Greek and Egyptian gods. As he thought more about the city, his enthusiasm for the project grew.

Plutarch tells of an incident that occurred as Alexander was marking the layout of his new city. Finding no chalk dust to use, he grabbed a handful of grain, and in the dirt he carefully drew the plans for his future city. However, a flock of birds came and ate every bit. Again, the king was worried, for this seemed to him a bad omen for the project.

Alexander consulted with his soothsayers, who, according to Plutarch, "urged him to take heart and interpreted the occurrence as a sign that the city would not only have abundant resources of its own, but would be the nurse of men of innumerable nations."[92]

As it turned out, the soothsayers had made a very accurate prediction. Alexandria, as it was named, was a beautiful city. Alexander drew up the plans for it himself and took a special interest in the layouts of the streets—a straight grid, which had not been part of other city plans. As Diodorus writes:

> By selecting the right angle of the streets, Alexander made the city breathe with the [northwestern winds of summer] so that as these blow across a great expanse of sea, they cool the air of the town, and so he provided its inhabitants with a moderate climate and good health.[93]

For more than a thousand years, Alexandria was a famous center of learning and culture, drawing scholars and artists from around the world.

"The Two-Horned One"

With Egypt completely in his control, some of Alexander's aides must have expected him to resume his military campaign, chasing down the elusive Darius in the east. However, Alexander had more urgent business, which would require a march through three hundred miles of desert.

The ancient historian Plutarch wrote biographies of famous people, including Alexander the Great.

It was an oracle—one as famous as the oracle at Delphi. This oracle was dedicated to the Egyptian god Ammon, sometimes referred to as Zeus-Ammon, since legend told that he was the son of the Greek god. Historians are unsure why Alexander needed to make the journey, but some speculate that ever since his mother had told him tales of his divine origins, he had been preparing for this time. Since his own ancestry could also be traced to Zeus, a meeting with the priest of Ammon could be very meaningful to the Macedonian king. Besides, his ancestor Hercules was said to have made the same pilgrimage centuries before.

His advisors, as usual, begged him to rethink his plans. The journey across the Libyan desert would be filled with danger. Sandstorms, the threat of dehydration, becoming hopelessly lost: all these were real possibilities. Why did he have to take such risks?

But Alexander was unshakable. As Plutarch writes, "The proud spirit which he carried into all his undertakings had created in him a passion for surmounting obstacles, so that in the end he was able to overcome not only his enemies but even places and seasons of the year."[94]

He was not bothered by storms or foul weather. He was lost once, but then was guided to safety by two cawing crows who flew overhead. Arrian agrees with Plutarch's assessment of Alexander's spirit and resolve, suggesting that perhaps the gods were on his side on that journey. "That some divine help was given him,"

writes the historian, "I can confidently as-set, because probability suggests it."[95]

Unlike his visit to Delphi, where the priests were not willing to speak with him, Alexander was greeted with warmth and respect by the priests of Ammon. They took him to their temple, for as he explained to them, he had important questions to ask the oracle. Exactly what these questions were has created much speculation among historians. Was he eager to find his true parentage? Did he want assurances that his new city would prosper, or that his battle against Darius would go well?

When he emerged from the sacred temple, he was quiet, saying only that he had received the answer his heart had desired. He wrote a long letter to his mother,

---

The Oracle of Ammon

Alexander's visit to the oracle of Zeus-Ammon in Libya was one of the most important experiences of his military campaign. The oracle was a mysterious force, which is described by Mary Renault in her book The Nature of Alexander.

"The oracle worked on a peculiar principle. . . . Originating in the Ammon temple at Thebes, its antiquity was immemorial. The symbol of the god, a round navel-shaped object, was carried in a kind of boat hung with precious vessels; long carrying poles rested on the shoulders of many priests. Under the god's direction they would turn, halt, or bow; from these movements the seer would read the god's response. (A similar ritual is still carried out in Alexandria by a Muslim sect, though of course without the idol; the devotees say that divine guidance comes as pressure on their shoulders.) This strange procession may have been visible from the courtyard. If he had indeed intended, as Arrian said, to declare what he had learned about himself, the solemn experience changed his mind. His sole comment was that he had had the answer his soul desired. He never told what the question was."

(Above) At the Ammon temple, priests warmly greet Alexander. Here, Alexander heard important prophecies. (Below) Alexander in the headdress of Ammon. He wore the headdress so often that many called him "The Two-Horned One."

telling her that the prophecies he heard were important, and that he would discuss them with her when he returned to Macedon. But he never returned home, and, since it is unlikely that he revealed the secrets to anyone else, he almost certainly carried the prophecies with him to his grave.

But there were rumors that Alexander had been assured that he was indeed the descendant of Zeus. And he fueled such rumors by proudly wearing the sacred headdress of Ammon, two ram's horns. He wore the headdress so often, in fact, that he was often referred to by the Egyptians and Greeks as "The Two-Horned One."

7 The New "Great King"

In spring of 331 B.C., after visiting the oracle, Alexander returned to Memphis. There his scouts reported that Darius had assembled a huge army—some witnesses estimated his force at one million soldiers—and was heading in their direction. Alexander and his men then moved east into Asia.

"I Will Not Steal My Victory"

Modern historians disagree as to the actual size of Darius's army. Many feel that the one-million tally is a gross exaggeration. Even so, they all agree that Alexander's 47,000-man army was vastly outnumbered, by at least four to one. In addition to his enormous legion of foot soldiers, Darius also used a large cavalry, a squad of four-horse chariots, and even elephants from India, whose purpose was to frighten the Macedonians' horses.

Darius was determined to crush Alexander's army. He knew that to be successful, he could not make the same errors in judgment he had made at Issus. He would not allow himself to be trapped

Persian archers as they may have looked in Alexander's day. While historians disagree as to the actual size of the Persian army, they do agree that Alexander's forces were vastly outnumbered.

The Confidence of a King

Plutarch relates an incident that took place before Alexander's battle against Darius at Gaugamela. As the anecdote shows, the Macedonian king had total confidence in the ability of his army to be successful—a confidence which surely inspired his soldiers.

"When his friends had gone, Alexander lay down in his tent and is said to have passed the rest of the night in a deeper sleep than usual. At any rate, when his officers came to him in the early morning, they were astonished to find him not yet awake, and on their own responsibility gave out orders for the soldiers to take breakfast before anything else was done. Then, as time was pressing, Parmenion entered Alexander's tent, stood by his couch and called him two or three times by name; when he had roused him, he asked how he could possibly sleep as if he were already victorious, instead of being about to fight the greatest battle of his life. Alexander smiled and said, 'Why not? Do you not see that we have already won the battle, now that we are delivered from roving around these endless plains, and chasing this Darius, who will never stand and fight?' And indeed not only beforehand, but at the very height of the battle Alexander displayed the supremacy and steadfastness of a man who is confident of the soundness of his judgement."

into a small space in which his armies were cramped and useless. The site of this battle would be a large plain near Gaugamela, in what is now northern Iraq.

As Alexander's army marched toward the battle site, Plutarch writes that his soldiers passed the time by staging mock battles: one side would pretend to be Darius, the other Alexander. When word of the fun came to Alexander's attention, he ordered that the leaders be matched as though they were fighting in individual competition. He even gave armor and a spear to the man who was playing Alexander. According to Plutarch, "The whole army watched this contest and saw in it something of an omen for their own campaign. After a strenuous fight, 'Alexander' finally prevailed, and received as a prize twelve villages."[96]

But the lighthearted mood quickly evaporated when the Macedonians arrived at Gaugamela. The size of Darius's army frightened them; Plutarch writes that the murmur of the Persian camp's voices was "like the distant roar of a vast ocean."[97] Some of Alexander's closest aides, the Companions, thought that perhaps they should attack the Persians that night. The element of surprise might nullify the advantage the huge army of Darius had over the Macedonians.

But Alexander vehemently opposed this idea. He knew that night battles were rarely decisive, for there were always more opportunities for the enemy to flee in the darkness. Splinter groups of the Persian army might very well disappear and come back to haunt the Macedonians another day. Besides, he wanted to show Darius that he was unafraid, and that no matter how large the Persian army, the Macedonians would be victorious. A nighttime battle would be less glorious, less courageous. "I will not steal my victory," Alexander proudly announced to the Companions.[98]

Instead of altering his plans, Alexander concentrated on inspiring his men. He spoke to them, reminding them how brave they had been in the past, and how they would surely be successful when the battle began the next morning. According to Ar-

rian, Alexander begged his men to remember how effective noise, or the absence of noise, could be to an enemy. He told them "to keep perfect silence when that was necessary in the advance, and by contrast to give a ringing shout when it was right to shout, and a howl to inspire the greatest terror when the moment came to howl."[99]

He also instructed them on a strategy to avoid the Persians' chariots. Darius considered them his most effective secret weapon, for they were equipped with razor-sharp curved knives on the wheels. They could cut the legs of the Macedonian cavalry horses or shred the flesh of Alexander's hoplites. So important were these chariots, in fact, that Darius had brought construction workers with him whose entire job was to prepare the battlefield for the chariots, smoothing out the

Alexander storms through the Persian line at Gaugamela. As he had at Issus, Darius fled in a panic.

A Greek frieze shows Alexander, drawn in a golden chariot, entering Babylon.

rough spots and removing stones that might upset the vehicles.

Alexander's plan was quite simple. He would position his army at an angle to the Persians. Darius would be forced to lead his charge, not over the smooth terrain he expected, but over rocky, bumpy ground. The dangerous chariots would have to go more slowly, and the Macedonians would repeat what they had done when Thracian rebels had rolled heavy wagons down an embankment at them—their ranks would part and the chariots would rumble between them.

That is precisely what happened. As the first gray lights of dawn filtered through the darkness, Alexander lined his men in what was for Darius an unexpected place. As the Great King charged, his chariots were lured over to bumpy, uneven ground where they were virtually harmless. The elephants, too, were kept from the Macedonians' horses by this maneuver.

The battle continued through the morning and into the afternoon. It was a frightful contest of two powerful armies, says Arrian, but in the end Darius ran, just as he had at Issus.

For a very little time it became a hand-to-hand fight, but when the cavalry with Alexander . . . pressed vigorously, shoving the Persians and striking their faces with their spears, and the Macedonian phalanx, solid and bristling with its pikes, had got to close quarters with them, and Darius, who had now long been in a panic, saw nothing but terrors all around, he was himself the first to turn and flee.[100]

To Babylon

After burying his dead and caring for his wounded, Alexander celebrated his victory. Twice he had met the Great King, and twice Darius had run after his army had been defeated. Alexander led the jubilant Macedonians on a 180-mile march south to Babylon, one of Darius's key cities. The Babylonian satraps had no intention of opposing Alexander, and they quickly surrendered their city. As Alexander and his men marched toward Babylon, trumpets and cymbals played, and the citizens threw pink and white flower petals in their path.

Alexander knew he would not find Darius here, for he knew from his scouts that the Persian had fled east, hoping to find what was left of his army and regroup. But there would be time for further battles later; for now, the Macedonians would get a much deserved rest. They admired the sights of the historic city, marvelling at the walls which ancient historians say were so thick that two four-horse chariots could pass one another on the top!

Because the city had been so quick to surrender and had given the Macedonians such a royal welcome, Alexander did not permit any plundering from citizens. The only wealth taken was from the royal treasury, by Alexander himself, and this he shared with his men. Most of them received a bonus equal to between two and ten months' pay for their loyalty and bravery in battle.

Alexander won the admiration of the priests of Babylon, for he continued his custom of respecting other cultures' religions. With the local holy men and sorcerers, he prayed and sacrificed to the Babylonian high gods, Baal and Marduk. Arrian writes that "whatever [the priests] directed him to do in regard to religious rites, he did." [101]

Adding Wealth

Alexander's next march was a long one—almost 375 miles southeast of Babylon to Susa, near the Persian Gulf. Susa was another of Darius's capitals, and the site of one of the Great King's largest treasuries. As in Babylon, Alexander was welcomed by both the citizens and local satraps, and in return, he spared their city violence. In Susa, Alexander left Darius's family, all of whom had traveled with the Macedonian army since the battle at Issus. Darius's family reportedly wept when Alexander left, for he had treated them so well.

While in Susa, Alexander received information that Darius was moving east across the northern part of Asia, trying to gather the remnants of his army to mount another attack. But Alexander was more interested in exploring the cities in the south, and so informed his men that they would be heading farther south, to the large city of Persepolis. Although Alexan-

Alexander makes a triumphant entry into Babylon. The Macedonians received a much deserved vacation in the beautiful old city.

Talking to Statues

In The Age of Alexander, *Plutarch tells of an incident that occurred when Alexander entered Persepolis. As was often the case, Alexander was ambivalent about the way he should conduct himself.*

"It was in Persepolis that Alexander saw a gigantic statue of Xerxes. This had been toppled from its pedestal and heedlessly left on the ground by a crowd of soldiers, as they forced their way into the place, and Alexander stopped and spoke to it as though it were alive. 'Shall I pass by and leave you lying there because of the expedition you led against Greece, or shall I set you up again because of your magnanimity and your virtues in other respects?' For a long while he gazed at the statue and reflected in silence, and then went on his way."

der had controlled his soldiers' looting and vandalism in the recent part of the campaign, Persepolis marked the end of that control. In fact, many historians suggest that the Macedonians' behavior at Persepolis was the beginning of the end for Alexander.

It is unknown whether Alexander planned to plunder and loot Persepolis, or to kill and murder its citizens. Not since the sieges of Tyre and Gaza had so much blood been shed. What happened in Persepolis was far worse, for this city did not oppose Alexander; like Babylon and Susa, it welcomed him.

A Hideous Sight

The trouble began before the Macedonians arrived in Persepolis. On the road they met a crowd of about eight hundred Greek slaves, most of them elderly. They had been mistreated by their Persian mas-

ters, and begging for mercy, had come to meet Alexander's army. Diodorus describes the slaves as a hideous, horrible sight. "All had been mutilated," he writes. "Some lacked hands, some feet, some ears and noses. They were men who had acquired skills or crafts and had made good progress in their instruction; then their other extremities had been amputated and they were left only those which were vital to their profession."[102]

The Macedonian soldiers, says Diodorus, pitied the men; Alexander could not restrain his tears. Alexander offered them safe passage back to Greece, assuming they would wish to return to their homeland. But the slaves were not interested in returning as freaks and oddities. They said they would rather remain in Persia, but would require land, money, tools, livestock, and seeds to set up their own village. Alexander gladly gave them everything they needed, then informed his men that Persepolis would be theirs to do with what they wished.

One of the most beautiful buildings in Persepolis had once belonged to Xerxes, pictured here with his queen. In a moment of drunken revelry, Alexander allowed the magnificent palace to be burned down.

The taking of Persepolis was not a battle. The gates to the city were open, for the people had heard of Alexander and had no wish to fight. But the citizens suffered one of the most savage acts of brutality in ancient history. Macedonian soldiers stormed through the city, rounding up people and murdering them. Anything that could be carried off was fair game— jewelry, money, household items. Women were raped and carried off to be raped again. Alexander's own share of the wealth was, according to Plutarch, so large that it took two thousand pairs of mules and five hundred camels to carry it back to Macedon.

Alexander occupied the city's royal palace, one of the most beautiful buildings in Persia. It had once belonged to Xerxes, the Persian general who had invaded Greece centuries before. Its murals, cedar pillars, and intricate detailing were legendary throughout the kingdom. But in a moment of drunken revelry, Alexander allowed the palace to be burned down; he even participated in starting the fire, by some accounts. His general Parmenio urged him not to do it, for it would show very bad judgment. According to Arrian, Parmenio argued "that it was not good to destroy what was now his own property, and that the Asians would not so readily adhere to him, but would suppose that even he had not decided to retain the empire of Asia, but only to conquer and pass on." [103]

But Alexander disregarded Parmenio's warnings, and allowed one after another of his drunken dinner guests to throw torches in the palace. Historians differ on whose idea it was—some say the lover of one of his soldiers suggested it as the ultimate revenge on Xerxes, others say Alexander himself thought of it. Whoever had the idea, it was Alexander who allowed it to become reality. Although he is said to have repented later, the action did not sit well with many of the king's most loyal admirers. Arrian, who rarely wrote a critical word about Alexander, thought that revenge against Xerxes, dead hundreds of years, was a poor motive for a foolish act. "I, too, do not think that Alexander showed good sense in this action," he wrote, "nor that he could punish Persians of a long time past."[104]

"You Are Making Them All the Equals of Kings"

Besides lamenting his poor judgment at Xerxes' palace, Alexander had another problem, one that surfaced at Persepolis and was growing day by day. His soldiers were acquiring massive amounts of wealth, thanks primarily to their king's generosity. However, that wealth was making them greedy and lazy. So much money was circulating within the Macedonian camp that merchants and traders set up a market which followed Alexander's men on their campaign. Says one historian, "The market that followed him was like a capital city's—anything could be bought there, were it rare as bird's milk."[105]

One of Alexander's men, Hagnon, was so wealthy he decided that the only boots that he would wear would be those made with nails of pure silver. Leonnatus, another officer, began using expensive powder on his body for wrestling. The powder was so unique, in fact, that it had to be imported via camel from Egypt. Perhaps the most excessive display of wealth was by Philotas, the son of General Parmenio. Philotas enjoyed hunting and gave himself the unbelievable advantage over his prey by ordering a woven net twelve miles across, which would trap the animals he flushed out of the forests!

Olympias wrote her son letters warning him of the danger of letting his men become too wealthy. "I wish you would find other ways of rewarding those you love and honor," she said. "As it is, you are making them all the equals of kings."[106]

Alexander agreed with his mother and worried about the situation, too. He tried on a number of occasions to remind the men of their humble origins and to encourage them to put less emphasis on material things. He also told them, according to Plutarch, that "he was amazed to see that men who had fought and conquered in such great battles could have forgotten that those who labor sleep more sweetly than those who are labored for."[107]

After spending the winter in Persepolis, Alexander was ready to begin a new campaign in the spring—this time to find Darius. There were rumors that the Great King had been captured by one of his own governors, Bessus, the satrap of Bactria. According to reports, Bessus had proclaimed himself the new Great King and was assembling an army.

Alexander's announcement to his men that they were about to leave the comforts of Persepolis was not a popular one. Nor was the march itself—more than four hundred miles in eleven days. The men grumbled a bit, but for the most part, Alexander was still a master of inspiration, motivating his men to do things they might not have believed they could accomplish.

A famous example of Alexander's leadership ability occurred on this long and difficult march. His men were hot and thirsty; most were severely dehydrated. Alexander, too, was faint from lack of water. At one point, the army met up with some men whose mules were loaded down with skins of water from a river. According to Plutarch, the men saw that Alexander was on the verge of collapse and quickly offered him a helmet full of water. Alexander took it, and

> then he looked up and saw the rest of his troops craning their heads and casting longing glances at the water, and he handed it back without drinking a drop. He thanked the men who had brought it to him, but said, "If I am the only one to drink, the rest lose heart."[108]

Such an action had a profound influence on his men. "They spurred on their horses and declared that they could not feel tired or thirsty or even like mortal men, so long as they had such a king."[109]

The Death of Darius

In a desert near the Caspian Sea, Alexander's scouts, who had ridden ahead of the Macedonian army, found Darius. Bessus's men had ambushed the Great King. He was bloody from numerous spear wounds and near death. He was moaning and begging for water when they came upon him.

The scouts hurried back to tell Alexander, but by the time he reached Darius, the Great King was dead. Alexander laid his own royal purple cloak over Darius's body and ordered that the body be taken back to Susa, where Darius's family was staying. There the Great King would be given a proper funeral.

It may seem odd that Alexander would take such care of a dead king who had been his enemy in life. But Darius was a king—unlike Bessus, who had once been Darius's trusted official, and who dared to steal the throne by ordering the murder of the king. As far as Alexander was concerned, the title of Great King of the Persian Empire belonged to him, not Bessus. Alexander's first priority was to hunt down Bessus and punish him for the murder of Darius.

Growing Discontent

But the plan was not as attractive to the Macedonian soldiers as it was to their king. They were growing tired of war; most had been away from home for four-and-a-half years. They had marched through Greece, Asia Minor, Africa, and Asia—more than seven thousand miles in all. Furthermore, what started out as a mission to avenge the long-ago Persian invasion of Greece had escalated to something very different. It was no longer a military campaign about Greek honor; it was a personal quest that really belonged just to Alexander.

Although his men still trusted him, they were growing annoyed with him. For one thing, he seemed to be turning into a Persian. He had started to wear many of the Persian styles, including long purple-and-white robes with sashes and ornate

Alexander bids farewell to his longtime enemy, Darius.

headdresses. He even wore the same kind of shoes the Persians favored, with space inside to add material to make the wearer look taller. And to the dismay of many of his supporters, he even made his Companions dress this way, too!

Alexander also seemed to like many of the Persian people, and this bothered some of his men. As was always his custom, Alexander left each conquered city in the hands of a local official whom he felt he could trust. Many of the Macedonians were jealous, feeling that their king should reward them not only with money, but also with power over these newly ac-

quired cities. Persian soldiers were even infiltrating the army and this infuriated many of the Macedonians. Although Hephestion and a few of Alexander's most loyal aides tried to be supportive and faithful, they could not sway the majority, who were less than happy with their king.

A Plot and Death

Alexander explained to his soldiers that they would not be going home just yet, but instead would be going eastward, to hunt

Despite what many anticipated, Alexander treated the slain king with honor: He covered Darius with his own cloak and ordered that the body be taken to Darius's family in Susa.

down Bessus. They would be foolish to end their campaign now, he said, for Bessus and his followers represented a dangerous threat to everything they had accomplished in the last four years. To leave Persia now would be throwing it all away.

The men followed, although they grumbled and muttered a great deal. Alexander was aware of this, and according to historians, he changed because of it. He became increasingly distrustful of his army. As one historian writes, "He drank a great deal at banquets, and listened increasingly to flatterers. His suspicions focused on anyone with a large following in the army."[110] The atmosphere in the camp was volatile; it probably seemed that any incident could have sparked an explosion.

The spark occurred during the winter of 330 B.C. While the army was resting in

Drangiana (present-day Afghanistan) Alexander received a report that there was a plot against his life by his own men. According to this report, one of his Companions, Philotas, the son of General Parmenio, knew of the plot but had not reported it to Alexander. Did this mean that Philotas himself was involved?

Philotas had been an annoyance to Alexander for some time. He was a boastful, arrogant young man, quick to mock or criticize others. He had recently remarked to other soldiers criticizing Alexander that "all the greatest achievements in the campaign had been the work of his father and himself," writes Plutarch. "Then he would speak of Alexander as a mere boy who owed his title of ruler to their efforts." [111]

When Alexander heard that Philotas had heard of the plot and said nothing, he was furious. Philotas did not deny hearing about the plot, but insisted that he thought it was just talk among disgruntled men; it was not to be taken seriously. Had he known the men were plotting in earnest, he said, he would have reported it immediately.

Not satisfied with Philotas's story (perhaps because of his personal dislike for the young man) Alexander called a council of advisors to try Philotas. Philotas was found guilty of participating in a plot to

The Tears of a Slave

The ancient historian Diodorus of Sicily tells of an occurrence when Alexander first entered Darius's palace in Susa. Alexander's reaction to a Persian slave's tears show an interesting side of the king's character.

"[Alexander] seated himself upon the royal throne, which was larger than the proportions of his body. When one of the pages saw that his feet were a long way from reaching the footstool which belonged to the throne, he picked up Darius's table and placed it under the dangling legs. This fitted, and the king was pleased by the aptness of the boy, but a slave standing by was troubled in his heart at this reminder of the changes of Fortune and wept. Alexander noticed him and asked, 'What wrong have you seen that you are crying?' The slave replied, 'Now I am your slave as formerly I was the slave of Darius. I am by nature devoted to my masters, and I was grieved at seeing what was most held in honor by your predecessor now become an ignoble piece of furniture.'

This answer reminded the king how great a change had come over the Persian kingdom. He saw that he had committed an act of arrogance . . . and calling the page who had placed the table, ordered him to remove it."

kill his king and was executed. It was customary at the time to kill not only a traitor, but his family and close friends as well. So old, loyal General Parmenio, who had been a close advisor to both Alexander and his father, was also killed. To the king's stunned troops, it was becoming clear that their king was not the same young man who used inspiring speeches and boundless generosity as tools to control his fighting men. Terror was replacing enthusiasm. Thus, in the early spring of 329 B.C., when Alexander asked them to march northeast in search of Bessus, they followed. It was not wise to oppose him.

Crossing the Hindu Kush

To find Bessus, the Macedonians had to cross a treacherous mountain range called Hindu Kush. It was their most difficult march. The steep, rocky terrain made it impossible for them to use their carts and wagons for supplies, so the men had to carry the provisions they needed. Many froze from the bitter cold and icy wind; many more were struck by snow blindness, caused by the dazzlingly bright surroundings. The thin air at eleven thousand feet made them dizzy, ill, and constantly tired. They ran short of food and other supplies, and because they were so far above the timber line, there was no fuel for their fires. The men existed by cutting up mules and eating the raw meat.

But marching in the bitter cold of the early spring paid off. Bessus was certain that Alexander would wait until the late spring thaw to cross the mountains and was totally unprepared for the Macedonian attack. He scrambled madly to cross

the Oxus River, burning his ferryboats behind him. Bessus trusted that the three-quarter-mile-wide river and its fast current would slow down the Macedonians, but they had met a similar challenge before. Alexander and his men stuffed their tents with straw and sewed them together to make them watertight. They crossed the river in just five days and quickly captured Bessus.

Alexander felt none of the respect for Bessus that he had for Darius. When the first Macedonian troops captured the satrap, they sent back word to Alexander and asked how Bessus should be brought into his presence. The king was very specific. According to Arrian, "Alexander ordered [them] to bring Bessus bound, naked, and wearing a wooden collar, and set him on the right of the road by which Alexander and his army were to pass."[112]

But Bessus's punishment went far beyond humiliation. He was tortured and whipped almost to the point of death. His nose and ears were cut off, and in a quick trial, was found guilty of murdering Darius. His hands and feet were bound to two saplings bent to the ground. As the guilty verdict was read, two soldiers slashed the ropes holding the trees close to the ground, and Bessus was ripped in half, the customary punishment for crimes against the Persian Empire.

Although Bessus was dead, there were other rebels in the northern regions of the empire who could mount threats to Alexander's throne. During the next several months, Alexander led his army through what would eventually become part of the Soviet Union. By 328 B.C., most of the empire seemed manageable, although morale in Alexander's camp was at an all-time low.

Bessus suffers the consequences of his betrayal of King Darius.

Alexander was less approachable to his men; he seemed suspicious and distrustful, even of the Companions. He seemed to enjoy large banquets more and more, and he drank heavily. Alexander also appeared to enjoy the company of flatterers: those who compared him to the greatest warriors in history, or better yet, to the gods. Worst of all, Alexander was beginning to believe such comparisons and to insist on divine treatment from his men. What was wrong, he wondered, with expecting his soldiers to bow down to him?

For the Persians, it was easy. It was customary in their empire to grovel before their king, lying on their stomachs while awaiting royal permission to stand in his presence. But to the Greeks and Macedonians, such a practice was almost laughable. They did not look on their kings as deities; kings were mortal men who occasionally made mistakes. To prostrate themselves before a king would be humiliating.

But for Alexander, the whole issue was a thorny one. Although he would have liked all his subjects to lie face down when they greeted him (a practice known as *proskynesis*) he knew his own men were scornful. But how could he expect the Persians to do it when his own countrymen refused? His authority might be undermined, and that was unthinkable to Alexander.

"You Scum!"

The issue of *proskynesis* and Alexander's pride came to violence in the fall of 328 B.C. at one of Alexander's banquets. Cleitus, one of the most loyal Companions, became drunk and began criticizing the king. He accused Alexander of disowning his father Philip so that he could claim to be a descendant of Zeus-Ammon.

Alexander would not tolerate criticism and lashed out at Cleitus. "You scum!" he cried. "Do you think you can keep on speaking to me like this, and stir up trouble among the Macedonians and not pay for it?"[113]

Cleitus was not afraid of Alexander and continued his criticism. Some historians say that he had been very close to Parmenio and Philotas and hated Alexander for putting them to death. Whatever the immediate cause of his outburst, he ridiculed Alexander for adopting Persian dress and for insisting on *proskynesis*, for wanting to be surrounded only with flatterers. He said that perhaps he should not "invite to his table free-born men who spoke their minds; it would be better for [Alexander] to spend his time among barbarians and slaves, who would prostrate themselves before his white tunic and his Persian girdle."[114]

He reminded Alexander that he was where he was only by the blood of Macedonians, and that he owed them a debt of gratitude. But Alexander was not interested in hearing about his debts to soldiers. Furious beyond reason, he pelted Cleitus with apples from a nearby dish. When Cleitus only laughed, Alexander grabbed a bodyguard's spear and ran it through Cleitus, killing him instantly.

Alexander despairs after drunkenly killing his friend Cleitus, an act that estranged him from his people.

A Different Sort of Man

Plutarch writes that Alexander repented almost immediately. When he came to his senses and saw the Companions staring at him, speechless, "he snatched the weapon out of the dead body and would have plunged it into his own throat if the guards had not forestalled him by seizing his hands and carrying him by force into the chamber."[115]

For three days and nights, Alexander sat in his tent, not moving or touching food or drink. The Companions were concerned. Here they were, thousands of miles from home, with a king who seemed bent on starving himself to death. What would become of them? The solution, as it turned out, was another trial. In a quick meeting, the Macedonian officers tried the dead Cleitus and found him guilty of treason. He had deserved to die, they decreed, and informed Alexander of their verdict. Somewhat cheered by their support of his deed, the king gradually came around and began planning his next campaign.

But his men were deeply concerned. They knew what had really happened: that one of their own had paid with his life for a few honest remarks to their king. The king, who had once endeared himself to his men through his impulsive generosity and stirring speeches, had been replaced by a different sort of man. They would have to be more careful.

8 Marching Off the Map

The people Alexander and his men encountered in the northernmost areas of the Persian Empire were far different from those they had met before. These were tribes of warriors, fiercely independent, whose remote villages were rarely visited by outsiders. They had resisted Darius and had no intention of knuckling under to a new Great King. Alexander would have to prove his superiority, for they were not awed by his reputation.

Soldiers with Wings

Alexander and his men marched north to Sogdiana, through bitter cold. Historians estimate that two thousand Macedonian soldiers died on the march from either exposure or pneumonia. The district was ruled by Oxyartes, a prince who had evacuated his village to take refuge atop a steep, rocky cliff. Satisfied that they were safe from the invading Macedonians, Oxyartes' warriors were amused by Alexander's offer to treat them kindly if they would surrender.

When Alexander's officers warned the warriors that they planned to attack the cliff, they were ridiculed. Writes Arrian, "They told Alexander with barbaric laugh-

ter to look for soldiers with wings to capture the mountain for him."[116] These "barbarians," as Arrian refers to them, were obviously not aware that Alexander and his men could rise to such a challenge.

At this stage in his campaign, Alexander found that offering rewards was a good incentive for his troops. He spoke to them all, pledging cash bonuses to the first hundred men who could scale the cliff walls. Many took him up on his offer.

Using hammers and tent pegs to chisel out toeholds in the rock, thousands of brave climbers began scaling the wall. Arrian reports that at least thirty died making the ascent, and "their bodies were not even found for burial, having fallen in different parts of the snow."[117] But several hundred men did reach the top, to the shock of Oxyartes' dozing guards. Alexander had given strict orders for his men to announce that they were the "soldiers with wings" needed for the battle. With almost no opposition, the Macedonians subdued the cliff warriors.

This episode had lingering importance, at least for Alexander's personal life. At a victory banquet, Oxyartes introduced Alexander to his daughter Roxane, who was said to be the loveliest woman in the empire, next to Darius's wife. Alexander fell in love with Roxane on the spot, say some historians, and promptly married her. It is noteworthy, however, that other historians maintain that the marriage was one of convenience rather than passion. They base that idea on two facts: Roxane is not mentioned among ancient historians for another four years, and Oxyartes was chosen to be Alexander's governor in the northern regions. A marriage was a common method of cementing bonds of political loyalty.

Where Else to Go?

After his victory over Oxyartes, Alexander took stock of his situation. He had dominated the western, northern, and southern regions of the Persian Empire, and he was still not satisfied. He turned to the eastern boundaries, toward India, as his final campaign. India had been part of Darius's empire for a short while, but the

The marriage feast of Alexander and Roxane. Historians disagree if this union stemmed from love or politics.

Great King had been unable to maintain control there. If Alexander could conquer India, he believed, he could truly say he was the most powerful ruler of all time.

Interestingly, Alexander's ideas of Indian and Asian geography were far different from reality. To the ancient Greeks, who wrote most of the geography books at the time, India was a narrow peninsula half its correct size. India was believed to be the easternmost boundary of Asia, bordered by Outer Ocean, the mysterious water that signalled the end of the earth. Alexander knew nothing of China, Malaysia, or any other Far East kingdoms. In his mind, the River Indus, which was the northern boundary of India, flowed directly into the Nile. He surmised this because both rivers contained crocodiles!

Although Alexander's geography was inaccurate, his enthusiasm soared as he prepared for his invasion of India. Assembling his largest army yet (close to 120,000 soldiers) he set out in the spring of 327 B.C. For the march, he decided to split his forces; half would go on the main road to India with Hephestion. When they reached the River Indus, they would build a bridge for easy crossing. Alexander

The Omen of Oil

Alexander's belief in omens meant that his soothsayers had to be ready at all times to interpret any unusual event, for the king feared that it might have a negative effect on his own plans. Before his invasion of India, such an occurrence was brought to the attention of the king and his fortune-tellers. This time, however, Alexander was hopeful that the omen was a good one, as Plutarch explains.

"The head of Alexander's household servants, a man named Proxenus, was digging a place to pitch the royal tent by the bank of the river Oxus, when he uncovered a spring of a smooth and fatty liquid. When the top of this was strained off, there gushed forth a pure and clear oil which appeared to be exactly like olive oil both in odor and in taste, and was also identical in smoothness and brightness, and this too in a country where there were no olive trees. It is said that the water of the Oxus itself is extraordinarily soft and gives a glossy texture to the skin of all those who bathe in it. It is clear that Alexander was delighted with this portent, if we may judge from a letter he wrote to Antipater, in which he speaks of it as one of the greatest signs of favor ever granted to him by the gods. The diviners, however, interpreted the omen as forecasting a campaign which would be a glorious one but also arduous and painful, for oil, they pointed out, was given to men by the gods as a refreshment for their labours."

would take the best archers and the phalanx troops and would circle north, subduing rebellious tribes that could be a problem to the Macedonians later.

Burning Baggage

Almost immediately, Alexander realized he had to make some drastic adjustments in his march. No longer was his army a lean, trim force of fighting men. Now they were heavily laden with wagonloads of plunder and spoils from their victorious battles. Their progress would be very slow unless they rid themselves of their heavy load.

Alexander's solution was dramatic—he set fire to his own baggage train and urged others to do the same. Few dared to refuse, says Plutarch, for "by this time he was already feared by his men for his relentless severity in punishing any dereliction of duty." His men burned their loot, too, "the great majority cheering with delight and raising their battle-cry."[118]

The march east along the northern frontier included one battle after another. Although in the past Alexander had shown leniency to tribes or cities that had fought gallantly, he was now merciless with every enemy. From the beginning of this campaign, writes one historian, "he considered the inhabitants as his subjects, expecting immediate submission and punishing resistance with massacre and enslavement."[119]

When his forces met up with Hephestion's at the River Indus, they crossed into surprisingly friendly territory. A rajah, or prince, named Taxiles greeted them and promised to support Alexander in his efforts if only he would help Taxiles defeat another rajah named Porus. Alexander

Alexander on his march toward India. For this campaign, he assembled his largest army to date.

was delighted for the support and promised his help. The Macedonian forces established a base in Taxiles' territory, planning their strategy against Porus, who was reported to be a wily, brave general.

To the Hydaspes

Early in May 326 B.C., Alexander led his men toward Porus's kingdom, a large territory on the other side of the Hydaspes River (now known as the Jhelum). The Macedonians were tense and jumpy; they had heard stories about Porus which frightened them. He was thought to be huge—some said he was almost seven feet tall. He had a massive cavalry and two hundred elephants who were trained to obey the commands of their riders.

Porus had deep respect for Alexander, although he knew the king by reputation

How to Catch Monkeys

When they were in India, Alexander and his men saw many animals they had never seen before. The monkey especially intrigued them, as well as the methods the Indians used to catch the creatures, as Diodorus describes.

"There were also many varieties of monkey, differing in size, which had themselves taught the Indians the method of their capture. They imitate every action that they see, but cannot well be taken by force because of their strength and cleverness. The hunters, however, in the sight of the beast, smear their eyes with honey, or fasten sandals about their ankles, or hang mirrors about their necks. Then they go away, having attached fastenings to the shoes, having substituted birdlime [a gluelike substance] for honey, and having fastened slip nooses to the mirrors. So when the animals try to imitate what they had seen, they are rendered helpless, their eyes stuck together, their feet bound fast, and their bodies held immovable. That is the way in which they become easy to catch."

only. He kept careful watch from his side of the river, even stationing long lines of elephants along the bank. He knew that if Alexander attempted to cross the river, the horses would bolt when they caught sight of the huge elephants.

When Alexander made camp on the opposite side of the river, he was impressed by the large number of soldiers in Porus's army. The fact that his soldiers were outnumbered would make Alexander's job more difficult. Another worry was the weather. It was monsoon season, with heavy rains and roaring winds. The monsoons would make crossing the Hydaspes—no easy feat even in pleasant weather—very difficult.

Throughout his military career Alexander had relied on the element of surprise. This was no exception. He directed his men to look and act busy, as if they were preparing boats for a river crossing. The Indian troops watched every move the Macedonians made. But nothing happened. There was no river crossing that day, or the next, or the next. Although Alexander's troops acted busy, they stayed on the other side of the river. Alexander even brought in wagonloads of supplies to make it seem as though they planned to be camped a long time.

After days of watching the activity across the river, the Indians grew indifferent. Clearly the Macedonians were being realistic and would wait for the torrents of wind and rain to stop before venturing across the river to attack. The Indian guards were no longer expecting anything; they were bored and tired of watching.

This was precisely what Alexander was waiting for. On a stormy, moonless night when Porus's guards were particularly inattentive, he and his men traveled eighteen miles upstream and crossed quickly in boats they had hidden in the brush. When the Macedonians attacked, Porus and his men were not prepared.

Frightening the Elephants

Porus tried to recover, and his troops busied themselves getting in formation. The elephants, his most powerful weapon, moved toward the Macedonian line, their drivers shouting commands and hurrying them on. Fearing his horses would become skittish if they saw the elephants, Alexander ordered the cavalry to stay back, behind the foot soldiers. Some of these hoplites were trodden underfoot, reports Diodorus, "armor and all, by the beasts, and they died, their bones crushed. Others were caught up by the elephants' trunks and, lifted on high, were dashed back down to the ground again, dying a fearful death."[120]

Protected by the solid wall of the Macedonian phalanx, more than one thousand

King Porus inspects his elephant troops (left). Rumors about the ferocity of these massive beasts terrified Macedonian soldiers. In battle, however, the elephants buckled under a rain of javelins and spears. Maddened with pain, the huge beasts became disoriented and trampled Porus's own foot soldiers (right).

archers on horseback fired arrows and spears at the elephants' riders, picking them off one by one. Soon Porus's powerful weapon turned out to be his own undoing. As the elephants became targets of the Macedonian spears and javelins, they became disoriented. One historian reports that the beasts were in such pain that they retreated step by step, giving out a high-pitched whistle, a noise made by rapping the tips of their trunks on the ground.

When brought before Alexander, the wounded Porus asked to be treated "as a king."

Without their riders and bleeding heavily from their sensitive trunk area, the elephants became wild, retreating in confusion and trampling the Indian foot soldiers around them. When this happened, Porus' ranks broke, and the battle was over. The rajah was captured and brought before Alexander.

Alexander's question to Porus was very direct. "How do you want to be treated?" he asked. Porus's answer was short and to the point, according to Plutarch. "As a king." When Alexander asked him to be more specific, Porus answered, "Those words include everything."[121] The Great King apparently was pleased with Porus's replies, for he allowed the rajah to continue governing his own kingdom and even added territory to it. As for the feud between Porus and Taxiles, historians say that Alexander was able to help them settle their differences and was supportive to them both.

Alexander mourned one casualty of the battle with all his heart. His horse Bucephalas, whom he had ridden since he was a boy, died of wounds and exhaustion. The horse was almost thirty years old, but that did not make his death any easier for Alexander to handle. As Plutarch writes, "He was plunged into grief . . . and felt that he had lost nothing less than a friend and a comrade."[122] In his memory, Alexander founded a new city, Bucephala, on the banks of the Hydaspes River.

Knowing When to Stop

The Macedonians engaged in small skirmishes after that, but none approached the size of the battle near the Hydaspes River. Alexander seemed energized after

The legendary duo preserved in bronze. Horse and rider were so close that when Bucephalas died, Alexander founded a city, Bucephala, in his memory.

his victory and was delighted when he and his men came within sight of the vast Himalayan Mountains. What lay beyond?

The Macedonian troops shared none of Alexander's enthusiasm or curiosity. They were tired of fighting battles, only to see Alexander give the enemy leaders independence after they were conquered. Why were they risking their lives for such meaningless wars? They were marching thousands of miles in stifling heat and what seemed like constant rain. More Macedonian soldiers were dying of fevers and infections than of enemy arrows.

Besides, the soldiers had heard rumors that giants lived beyond those great mountains, with armies made up of thousands of elephants. They were not interested in meeting such an enemy face-to-face. So when the army reached the Beas River, and Alexander was making plans to cross it to continue his march, the soldiers refused. They had had enough. They wanted to go home.

Alexander was sympathetic. He had seen the morale sag before and knew that he could always rally the men with a stirring speech appealing to their courage and honor. But not this time. His speech was a good one, but not good enough. When he finished talking, old Coenus, a veteran officer, stepped forward.

He spoke for the men, he told Alexander. He urged his king not to be a leader of unwilling troops; it was important for a leader to know when to stop. Alexander should go home, see his mother, and tend to the affairs of the Greeks. If afterwards he wanted to return to India, said Coenus, he should take "young men in place of old, men who are fresh and not worn out. . . . It is likely that they will follow you with all the more enthusiasm."[123] As for these men, he said to Alexander, they wanted to go home to their families, to enjoy the victories they had earned.

The men who were listening were moved by his words. Arrian writes that Coenus's speech "produced uproar among the audience and that many even shed tears."[124] Alexander, however, was not pleased, and stormed off to his tent to sulk. For three days he stayed in his tent, refusing to talk to anyone. Although in the past his officers had tried to please him and had worried about his angry moods, this time they remained firm. Historian Mary Renault says that "they answered sulk with sulk."[125]

In the end, Alexander understood that he could not persuade the men to continue. He called in his soothsayers, asking them what the omens said about continuing his march. Perhaps to save face for their king, the soothsayers were in agreement when they announced that the omens looked quite bad. It would be better to turn back. Satisfied, Alexander announced to his troops that they would be returning home.

Morale at its Lowest

When Alexander's army refused to go any farther into India, they were protesting conditions that had been plaguing them ever since entering that territory. As Mary Renault explains in The Nature of Alexander, *the excitement of battle had been replaced by total physical discomfort.*

"By this time they had probably decided that it rained in India for nine or ten months a year. The miseries of constant soakings were made worse by inadequate clothes. They could well afford the good strong wool or linen they were used to, but when it wore out, they could get only wretched flimsy cotton, with no wear in it nor protection from the armor's chafing, tearing on every thorn; they referred to the stuff as 'Indian rags.' They were sick of trudging in pulp-wet boots through deep mud churned up by the column of lame horses with thrushy frogs and worn hooves; of heaving at the wheels of bogged-down ox carts; of moldy food, mildewed leather, and daily scourings of all their metal for rust. They felt no exhilaration at the thought of larger elephants, or new tribes of warriors, or the half-month march through desert which they heard would lie between."

Death seemed imminent when Alexander was wounded by an arrow that pierced his breastplate. This news sent shock waves through the Macedonian camp.

Rumors of Death

Although Alexander agreed to begin marching home, he did not intend to go home the same way he arrived. He was curious about where the Indus River met the sea, and he intended to find the answer. After having his carpenters build a fleet of ships, he ordered part of the army to sail south, toward the sea, the rest of the troops would march on land, as support.

The journey almost had a tragic end. While crossing a desert near the river rapids, Alexander and his men encoun-tered a tribe called the Malli, who were re-puted to be the most hostile and warlike of all Indians. The Malli were strong fight-ers and soon engaged the Macedonians in battle. At one point in the fight, Alexan-der felt that his men weren't being aggres-sive enough and dashed up a ladder to scale the Mallian city wall without his usu-al crowd of bodyguards. He hoped that by endangering himself, he would spur his soldiers to fight harder.

But as he climbed over the wall of the city, he was hit by an arrow that went through his breastplate and lodged in his chest. His ribs were crushed and his lung collapsed; Arrian writes that "breath as well as blood spouted from the wound."[126] Although he tried to continue fighting, he soon fainted, to the horror of his men.

He was carried off to a tent, where attendants sawed off the wooden shaft of the arrow and performed some quick surgery. "They had to cut out the arrowhead," writes Plutarch, "which was embedded between his ribs and measured . . . four fingers width in length and three in breadth."[127]

For days the king fought death, while rumors of his death spread like wildfire through the camp, some miles away. The men were frightened and worried. What would happen to them in this hostile, foreign land without Alexander? The possibilities were not comforting, based on the tribes they had met thus far. And although Alexander's officers tried to assure the men that he was not dead, the obvious absence of their king made such assurances meaningless.

After a week, it seemed as though Alexander would live. But the rumors continued, and since nothing but proof would convince his men that he was alive, he decided to show himself to the troops—much to the dismay of his doctors. Bodyguards carried him on a stretcher to the river, and he sailed down close to the camp. When they docked, his attendants offered to carry him on the stretcher again into the camp, but he refused. Nearchus, one of Alexander's men, later said, "He ordered a horse to be fetched him. And when he mounted it and everyone saw him, the whole army clapped their hands repeatedly, and the banks and river-glades threw back the sound."[128]

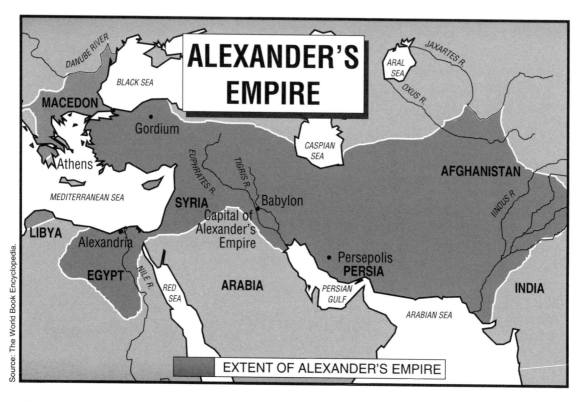

EXTENT OF ALEXANDER'S EMPIRE

Source: The World Book Encyclopedia.

The Mysterious People of Cedrosia

In his writings, the ancient historian Diodorus of Sicily tells of a strange group of people Alexander's army met while marching along the southern coast of the Persian Empire.

"Next Alexander advanced into Cedrosia, marching near the sea, and encountered a people unfriendly and utterly brutish. Those who dwelt here let the nails of their fingers and toes grow from birth to old age. They also let their hair remain matted like felt. Their color is burned black by the heat of the sun, and they clothe themselves in the skins of beasts. They subsist by eating the flesh of stranded whales. They build up the walls of their houses and construct roofs with whale's ribs, which furnish them rafters eighteen cubits in length. In the place of tiles, they covered their roofs with the scales of these beasts."

The Last March

By early autumn of 325 B.C. Alexander had regained his strength and busied himself planning a new way home. He had wondered for some time about whether a sea route between Persia and India existed; he decided to explore that possibility. Again he divided his troops into sailors and soldiers. Some would explore offshore, sailing along the coast. The rest (about ten thousand men) he would lead as support troops to the sailors. They would march along the coastline and provide fresh food and water to the sailors.

The ordeal was a nightmare from the beginning. After following the fleet for only one hundred miles, Alexander's army found the coastline terrain too rocky and difficult. They moved inland and continued their march in the desert. But the desert was even worse. The scorching heat and strong, hot winds blasted the men, making daytime marches impossible. Alexander saw how the men were struggling and decided to march only at night.

But while the darkness helped keep the temperature a bit cooler, it masked many of the desert's dangers, including thorn bushes "so savage they could drag a man from his horse," according to Arrian.[129] Also, the heat was taking such a toll on the men and animals that it did not seem to matter if they were resting or marching. Horses and mules were dropping dead from exhaustion and lack of water. And the desperate soldiers—many of whom had not had a drop of water in days—fell upon the dead animals, drinking their blood and taking a few scraps of flesh for food.

Food was almost as scarce as water in the desert. Besides feeding themselves, Alexander's men had the added responsibility of finding food for the sailors, too. In one instance, Alexander sent a squadron of men to the seashore, bringing boxloads of food for those on board the ships. But the starving soldiers could not resist the temptation: they broke open the boxes and ate the food themselves. Although the two divisions tried to maintain contact, a storm at sea forced the sailors from their schedule, and the marchers were not able to maintain contact for months.

Weeks turned into months for Alexander's troops. The loss of the horses and mules meant that the sick and injured could not be transported. Most of those who could not keep up dragged farther and farther behind, until they simply dropped. Arrian writes of thousands of men who "were lost in the sand, like men who fall overboard at sea."[130] After sixty days of wandering, the remainder of Alexander's army came to a city where there was water and food to revive the half-crazed men. Amazingly, three-fourths of Alexander's men had been lost on the Indian expedition—most of them on the trip back.

Forcing Unity

Alexander moved his troops to Susa for an extended stay. Most of his men were ill from heatstroke and dehydration; all were exhausted. Going home to Macedon was probably on the men's minds—but not Alexander's. Although he was keeping his promise of heading in the general direction of home, he was not taking a direct route. He was interested in seeing Italy, Spain, and more of North Africa. He even toyed with a plan to circumnavigate the entire African continent. But he knew he could never accomplish these campaigns with the small army he had left.

More help from the Persians was important, but that issue was turning into a touchy subject with his men. He had allowed some Persians to be officers and aides—even members of the Companions—and this angered many Macedonians. His love of Persian dress and customs was still strong, too, and it seemed to many of his soldiers that Alexander was betraying his heritage. "All this aggrieved the Macedonians," writes Arrian, "as they thought that Alexander was going utterly barbarian at heart."[131]

The last straw was the appearance of thousands of new soldiers for the Macedonian army—from Persia! Earlier in his Asian campaign, Alexander had ordered the selection of thirty thousand boys from various districts in Persia, based on strength and physical appearance. He wanted these boys trained to be good Greek and Macedonian soldiers, they were even to learn the Greek language. Now back in Susa, Alexander was informed that the boys were ready—that they had become skilled "Greek" soldiers worthy of Alexander's army. But Alexander's men resented these young outsiders, and became even more resentful when Alexander referred to the thirty thousand as "his successors."

Morale dropped from bad to worse in Susa. Alexander arranged Persian marriages for ninety of his officers and planned an elaborate ceremony so that all could be married at the same time. He himself married two Persian women in that ceremony—again, historians believe, to cement relations between the Greek and Persian governments. His best friend Hephestion was part of the ceremony. He married the sister of one of Alexander's wives, so, the king planned, their children could be cousins.

Begone!

Such actions enraged the Macedonian soldiers. They felt betrayed and used. It seemed, in Arrian's words, "as if Alexander was actually contriving every means of reducing his dependence on Macedonians in the future."[132] They felt jealous and demeaned. So when Alexander gave what he thought would be a popular announcement—that all of his older soldiers were released and could go home to Macedon—they exploded.

Had he no use for them, now that they had gone through hell and back for him? Did he now prefer the company of these fresh, young Persian men to his tough, old veterans? The assembled soldiers soon became a mob and hurled insults at Alexander. As Arrian writes, "They did not endure in silence, but called on him to discharge them all from the army, and to campaign himself in company with his father, referring in mockery to Zeus-Ammon."[133]

Stung by his men's hostility, Alexander leaped from the platform where he had been standing and gave a furious speech to his men. He told them that they could all discharge themselves, that was fine. But before they acted hastily, they should remember how he had raised them from the level of shepherds in the remote areas of Macedon to become conquerors. He reminded them, too, that he would match anyone in the amount of pain and suffering endured—he offered to strip and match them wound for wound. He finished:

> And now, as you all desire to go, let all of you begone, return to your homes and report that . . . you deserted your king and went off, handing him over to the protection of the barbarians he had conquered. This is a report that will perhaps win you a fine reputation with men, and will doubtless be holy in the sight of heaven. Begone![134]

Alexander stormed back to his tent leaving his soldiers speechless. They sent representatives to him to beg their king's forgiveness, but to no avail. Alexander was not interested in their guilt and their apologies. For two days and nights he brooded in his tent, refusing to see them. But, according to Plutarch, "the men would not go away and remained for two days and nights outside his tent weeping and calling him master."[135]

Finally Alexander accepted their fervent apologies. He called his men to him, and they hung their heads and threw

Ancient Persians had a distinct style of dress. Alexander's willingness to adopt Persian attire angered his men, who felt he was betraying his heritage.

down their spears and shields—a sign of surrender on the battlefield. They were sorry, they said, but it had hurt them when Alexander called the Persians his kinsmen and let them approach him as easily as the Macedonians.

Alexander's answer pleased the men. "But I regard all of you as my kinsmen, and from this time forth I shall give you that name." At that, the men came up one at a time, writes Arrian, and kissed him in the way kinsmen are permitted to greet their king. The men were both relieved and energized afterwards, according to the ancient text, for "they took up their arms again and returned to the camp shouting and singing their victory song."[136]

The Death of a Friend

Though Alexander and his men felt strong and confident after the events in Susa, the army never resumed its campaign. Not long afterwards, Hephestion became ill with a fever. He was under the care of a camp doctor, a Greek man named Glaucias. Glaucias had given Hephestion a strict diet to follow as long as he was ill, but the young soldier began to feel better and ignored the doctor's instructions. Plutarch reports that "he sat down to breakfast, devoured a boiled fowl and washed it down with a great cooler full of wine."[137] By that afternoon, Hephestion was dead.

Alexander was beside himself with grief. He wept for three days, and, feeling no better, ordered poor doctor Glaucias to be crucified. In a tribute to his friend, Alexander instructed the manes and tails of all the horses to be cut (a sign of mourning in ancient times). He also cut his own golden hair completely short, except for one long lock which he tied in a circle.

Alexander gave a flurry of commands to make certain the camp would pay proper respect to Hephestion. No music of any kind could be played in camp until further orders were given. All decorations

Alexander is overcome with grief over the death of his friend Hephestion.

Alexander's men bid him a somber goodbye moments before his death in 323 B.C.

and flags were taken off the city walls and campsites. Hephestion was to be honored by architects and sculptors who were to design shrines and statues for large cities around the empire.

Still feeling overwhelming grief, Alexander set off on a military campaign, as Plutarch writes, "as if the tracking down and hunting of men might console him, and he subdued the Cossaens [a mountain tribe], massacring the whole male population from youths upwards; this was termed a sacrifice to the spirit of Hephestion."[138]

It is ironic that Alexander, who wanted his and Hephestion's lives to be so closely entwined, followed his friend in death so soon. After moving west to Babylon in the early summer of 323 B.C., Alexander fell ill with a fever and stabbing stomach cramps. The illness soon turned to pneumonia, and the king hung on to life by a semi-conscious thread for eleven days. But his lungs were heavily damaged from earlier wounds, and they failed him. At the age of thirty-three, King Alexander of Macedon, Greece, Persia, Africa, and India was dead.

A Dreadful Legacy

Alexander's body was not yet cold when the wrangling over his empire began. Who would be the successor? How would such an awesome responsibility be handled?

Before he slipped into death, one of Alexander's generals gently asked the king to whom power should pass when he died. According to ancient historians, Alexander whispered, "To the strongest." But the answer was vague. Two of his wives were pregnant at the time. Did he mean to the strongest of the two heirs, yet unborn? Or did he intend for the crown to pass to anyone who was strong enough to take the challenge?

Chaos and Murder

The question was never really settled. As soon as he died, the empire fragmented, for no one seemed as capable as Alexander of holding it together. Chaos, murders, and plots to seize power abounded. Roxane, one of the pregnant wives, tried to protect the throne for her unborn child by having the other expectant wife murdered. And although Roxane's son (Alexander IV) survived for a time, protected by his grandmother Olympias, murder claimed him while he was still a young boy.

The legend of Alexander has inspired countless poets, painters, and sculptors.

Without an heir, Alexander's power passed to the military. Here again, no one man was strong enough to command the entire empire, so there was a great deal of jockeying for position and authority within various territories. "Each general and governor seized the power which Alexander's death left in his hands," writes historian Jacob Abbott, "and endeavored to defend himself in the possession of it against the others. Thus the devastation and misery which the making of these conquests brought upon Europe and Asia were continued for many years."[139]

In the end, three of Alexander's generals grabbed enough control to take over large chunks of the empire and govern them. Antigonus took Macedon, Ptolemy controlled Egypt and Libya, and Seleucus took charge of Babylonia and its surrounding territory. The rest of the empire was taken over by various local officials and satraps.

Historians have remarked that it was a tribute (although admittedly an ironic tribute) to Alexander's great personal glory that his empire could not survive his death. But the fragmentation and dismemberment of the empire he had worked so hard to gain raises interesting questions on Alexander's importance. Great men and women of history are usually measured by their lasting accomplishments; Alexander's accomplishments disappeared directly after his death. In one of the speeches Alexander gave to his soldiers, he said, "It is a lovely thing to live with courage, and to die, leaving behind an everlasting renown."[140] What was Alexander's "everlasting renown"?

In the absence of Alexander's great leadership, the empire crumbled. Seleucus, one of Alexander's generals, governed one chunk of the once-mighty empire.

Reconciler? Savage?

Some historians believe that Alexander's importance was in showing the world that cultures could exist side by side. They point to his willingness to adopt Persian ways and to urge his men to do the same. He allowed non-Greeks and non-Macedonians to assume high government posts in his empire and to be officers in his army.

Plutarch writes that

Alexander considered that he had come from the gods to be a general governor and reconciler of the world. Using force of arms when he did not bring men together by the light of reason, he harnessed all resources to one and the same end, mixing the lives, manners, marriages, and customs of men, as it were in a loving-cup.[141]

Alexander the Great—bloodthirsty tyrant or unifier of men?

But others see Alexander's accomplishments in a different light. They point to a twenty-thousand-mile trail of violence and destruction, all for no reason other than personal glory and accomplishment. "His business was war and conquest," writes historian Peter Green. "It is idle . . . to pretend that he dreamed, in some mysterious fashion, of wading through rivers of blood and violence to achieve the Brotherhood of Man."[142] Another historian agrees. "His dreadful legacy was to ennoble savagery in the name of glory, and to leave a model of command that far too many men of ambition sought to act out in the centuries to come."[143]

Indeed, if a peaceful unity of nations really was his goal, it would be difficult to prove it. Alexander died before he could demonstrate any ability to govern fairly or wisely, so we cannot know what sort of ruler he would have become. It is true, however, that Alexander seemed to take no interest in the affairs of territories once he had conquered them, and that he enjoyed the thrill of battle far more than the day-to-day drudgery of government. He was more than willing to leave politics to others. In addition, Alexander made no preparations for a transfer of power. Alexander's father Philip had tried very hard to teach his son military strategy. Although he was childless at his death, Alexander gave no special attention to any of his generals as possible successors.

Possibly the most important of Alexander's legacies was his extraordinary model for military leadership. He was a superb tactician and a bold field general. In all his battles he was at the front of the charge, setting an example for bravery and courage, without regard for his own life. And when it was necessary to inspire his men, he was very successful. With coaxing, wheedling, flattering, and at times, raw emotion, Alexander held remarkable power over his men, inspiring them to accomplish feats seemingly beyond their capabilities.

The results he and his army gained were nothing short of astonishing. At the time of his death, he had conquered the largest segment of the earth ever managed by one person. It was this power that captured people's imagination and admiration centuries later.

The Romans were the first to add "the Great" to Alexander's name, for they, too, tried to conquer a large mass of the earth. Conquerors like Louis XIV, Napoleon, and Adolf Hitler read of Alexander's exploits and praised him. Julius Caesar wept

Alexander's coffin depicts a battle between the Greeks and Persians. Whether his legacy is dreadful or admirable, few deny that it is anything short of astonishing.

when he reached his thirty-second birthday and had not accomplished as much as Alexander by that age. Poets, painters, and sculptors were inspired by him. Michelangelo even laid out the courtyard of the Vatican in Rome in the design of Alexander's shield.

War and conquest were considered worthy goals in the ancient times of Alexander. Whether his accomplishments in war are considered exemplary by today's standards is a far different matter.

Whether defeating millions of people and claiming territory on three continents is admirable is not the issue. As biographer W.W. Tarn writes, "For whatever else [Alexander] was, he was one of the supreme fertilizing forces of history. He lifted the civilized world out of one groove and set it in another. He started a new epoch; nothing could again be as it had been."[144] For good or bad, Alexander of Macedon became the standard by which ambitious men with armies are measured.

Notes

Introduction: King, Master, Pharaoh, God

1. Quoted in Charles Mercer, *Alexander the Great*. New York: American Heritage Publishing Co., 1962.
2. *Diodorus of Sicily, Book XVIII.* Translated by Russel M. Geer. Cambridge, MA: Harvard University Press, 1962.
3. *Diodorus of Sicily, Book XVIII.*
4. *Diodorus of Sicily, Book XVIII.*
5. Jacob Abbott, *History of Alexander the Great.* New York: Harper and Brothers, 1876.

Chapter 1: The Roots of an Earthshaker

6. C.L. Sulzberger, *Fathers and Children: How Famous Leaders Were Influenced by Their Fathers.* New York: Arbor House, 1987.
7. N.G.L. Hammond, *Alexander the Great: King, Commander, and Statesman.* Park Ridge, NJ: Noyes Press, 1980.
8. John W. Snyder, *Alexander the Great.* New York: Twayne Publishers, 1966.
9. Robin Lane Fox, *The Search for Alexander.* Boston: Little, Brown and Company, 1980.
10. A.B. Bosworth, *Conquest and Empire: The Reign of Alexander the Great.* Cambridge, England: Cambridge University Press, 1988.
11. Plutarch, *The Age of Alexander.* Translated by Ian Scott-Kilvert. Middlesex, England: Penguin Books, 1973.
12. Plutarch, *The Age of Alexander.*
13. Plutarch, *The Age of Alexander.*
14. Mary Renault, *The Nature of Alexander.* New York: Pantheon Books, 1975.
15. Renault, *The Nature of Alexander.*
16. Peter Green, *Alexander the Great.* New York: Praeger Publishers, 1970.
17. Plutarch, *The Age of Alexander.*
18. Plutarch, *The Age of Alexander.*
19. Quoted in Mercer, *Alexander the Great.*
20. Quoted in Renault, *The Nature of Alexander.*
21. Quoted in A.R. Burn, *Alexander the Great and the Hellenistic Empire.* New York: Macmillan, 1948.
22. Renault, *The Nature of Alexander.*

Chapter 2: From Soldier to King

23. Abbott, *History of Alexander the Great.*
24. Mercer, *Alexander the Great.*
25. Abbott, *History of Alexander the Great.*
26. *Diodorus of Sicily, Book XVI.*
27. Mercer, *Alexander the Great.*
28. Plutarch, *The Age of Alexander.*
29. Burn, *Alexander the Great and the Hellenistic Empire.*
30. Plutarch, *The Age of Alexander.*
31. Quoted in Green, *Alexander the Great.*
32. Plutarch, *The Age of Alexander.*
33. Green, *Alexander the Great.*
34. Plutarch, *The Age of Alexander.*

Chapter 3: Establishing Command

35. Burn, *Alexander the Great and the Hellenistic Empire.*
36. John Keegan, *The Mask of Command.* New York: Viking Press, 1987.
37. Keegan, *The Mask of Command.*
38. Plutarch, *The Age of Alexander.*
39. Mercer, *Alexander the Great.*
40. Mercer, *Alexander the Great.*
41. Arrian, *History of Alexander and Indica (Book I).* Translated by P.A. Brunt. Cambridge, MA: Harvard University Press, 1976.

42. Arrian, *History of Alexander and Indica.*

43. Green, *Alexander the Great.*

44. Green, *Alexander the Great.*

45. Plutarch, *The Age of Alexander.*

46. Abbott, *History of Alexander the Great.*

47. Arrian, *History of Alexander and Indica.*

48. Plutarch, *The Age of Alexander.*

49. Plutarch, *The Age of Alexander.*

Chapter 4: Taking On Persia

50. Quoted in Mercer, *Alexander the Great.*

51. Stephen Krensky, *Conqueror and Hero: The Search for Alexander.* Boston: Little, Brown and Company, 1981.

52. Quoted in Burn, *Alexander the Great.*

53. Fox, *The Search for Alexander.*

54. Quoted in Renault, *The Nature of Alexander.*

55. Keegan, *The Mask of Command.*

56. Snyder, *Alexander the Great.*

57. Fox, *The Search for Alexander.*

58. Agnes Savill, *Alexander the Great and His Time.* London: Rockliff Publishers, 1955.

59. Quoted in Arrian, *History of Alexander and Indica.*

60. Plutarch, *The Age of Alexander.*

61. Arrian, *History of Alexander and Indica.*

62. Quoted in Plutarch, *The Age of Alexander.*

63. Arrian, *History of Alexander and Indica.*

Chapter 5: Storming Across Asia

64. Renault, *The Nature of Alexander.*

65. Arrian, *History of Alexander and Indica.*

66. Quoted in *Greece and Rome: Builders of Our World.* Edited by Merle Severy. New York: National Geographic Society, 1968.

67. Arrian, *History of Alexander and Indica.*

68. Arrian, *History of Alexander and Indica.*

69. Arrian, *History of Alexander and Indica.*

70. Plutarch, *The Age of Alexander.*

71. Abbott, *History of Alexander the Great.*

72. Arrian, *History of Alexander and Indica.*

73. Arrian, *History of Alexander and Indica.*

74. Arrian, *History of Alexander and Indica.*

75. Arrian, *History of Alexander and Indica.*

76. Arrian, *History of Alexander and Indica.*

77. Plutarch, *The Age of Alexander.*

78. Plutarch, *The Age of Alexander.*

79. Quoted in Renault, *The Nature of Alexander.*

80. Plutarch, *The Age of Alexander.*

81. Plutarch, *The Age of Alexander.*

82. Plutarch, *The Age of Alexander.*

83. Savill, *Alexander the Great and His Time.*

84. Quoted in Mercer, *Alexander the Great.*

Chapter 6: From Tyre to Egypt

85. Arrian, *History of Alexander and Indica.*

86. Quoted in Abbott, *History of Alexander the Great.*

87. Abbott, *History of Alexander the Great.*

88. *Diodorus of Sicily,* Book XVI.

89. Mercer, *Alexander the Great.*

90. Green, *Alexander the Great.*

91. Bosworth, *Conquest and Empire: The Reign of Alexander the Great.*

92. Plutarch, *The Age of Alexander.*

93. *Diodorus of Sicily, Book XVII.* Translated by C. Bradford Welles. Cambridge, MA: Harvard University Press, 1963.

94. Plutarch, *The Age of Alexander.*

95. Arrian, *History of Alexander and Indica.*

Chapter 7: The New "Great King"

96. Plutarch, *The Age of Alexander.*

97. Plutarch, *The Age of Alexander.*

98. Quoted in Plutarch, *The Age of Alexander.*

99. Arrian, *History of Alexander and Indica.*

100. Arrian, *History of Alexander and Indica.*

101. Quoted in Mercer, *Alexander the Great.*

102. *Diodorus of Sicily,* Book XVII.

103. Arrian, *History of Alexander and Indica.*

104. Arrian, *History of Alexander and Indica*.

105. Quoted in Renault, *The Nature of Alexander*.

106. Quoted in Plutarch, *The Age of Alexander*.

107. Plutarch, *The Age of Alexander*.

108. Plutarch, *The Age of Alexander*.

109. Plutarch, *The Age of Alexander*.

110. Krensky, *Conqueror and Hero: The Search for Alexander*.

111. Plutarch, *The Age of Alexander*.

112. Arrian, *History of Alexander and Indica*.

113. Quoted in Plutarch, *The Age of Alexander*.

114. Plutarch, *The Age of Alexander*.

115. Plutarch, *The Age of Alexander*.

Chapter 8: Marching Off the Map

116. Arrian, *History of Alexander and Indica*.

117. Arrian, *History of Alexander and Indica*.

118. Plutarch, *The Age of Alexander*.

119. Bosworth, *Conquest and Empire: The Reign of Alexander the Great*.

120. *Diodorus of Sicily*, Book XVII.

121. Quoted in Plutarch, *The Age of Alexander*.

122. Plutarch, *The Age of Alexander*.

123. Quoted in Arrian, *History of Alexander and Indica*.

124. Arrian, *History of Alexander and Indica*.

125. Renault, *The Nature of Alexander*.

126. Arrian, *History of Alexander and Indica*.

127. Plutarch, *The Age of Alexander*.

128. Quoted in Renault, *The Nature of Alexander*.

129. Arrian, *History of Alexander and Indica*.

130. Arrian, *History of Alexander and Indica*.

131. Arrian, *History of Alexander and Indica*.

132. Arrian, *History of Alexander and Indica*.

133. Arrian, *History of Alexander and Indica*.

134. Arrian, *History of Alexander and Indica*.

135. Plutarch, *The Age of Alexander*.

136. Arrian, *History of Alexander and Indica*.

137. Plutarch, *The Age of Alexander*.

138. Plutarch, *The Age of Alexander*.

Epilogue: A Dreadful Legacy

139. Abbott, *History of Alexander the Great*.

140. Arrian, *History of Alexander and Indica*.

141. Plutarch, *The Age of Alexander*.

142. Green, *Alexander the Great*.

143. Keegan, *The Mask of Command*.

144. W.W. Tarn, *Alexander the Great*. Boston: Beacon Press, 1956.

For Further Reading

A.R. Burn, *Alexander the Great and the Hellenistic Empire*. New York: Macmillan, 1948. Interesting reading, especially about Alexander's boyhood.

Trevor Nevitt Dupuy, *The Military Life of Alexander the Great of Macedon*. New York: Franklin Watts, 1969. Good insights about Alexander's military strategies and descriptions of major battles.

Peter Green, *Alexander the Great*. New York: Praeger Publishers, 1970. Good photographs of ancient relics, easy reading.

Edith Hamilton, *The Echo of Greece*. New York: W.W. Norton, 1957. Good general overview of Alexander's importance.

N.G.L. Hammond, *Alexander the Great: King, Commander, and Statesman*. Park Ridge, NJ: Noyes Press, 1980. Although difficult reading, the book gives interesting details of Alexander's military life.

Stephen Krensky, *Conqueror and Hero: The Search for Alexander*. Boston: Little, Brown and Company, 1981. Very easy reading, excellent account of Alexander's early life.

Frank Lipsius, *Alexander the Great*. New York: Saturday Review Press, 1974. Good maps, valuable bibliography.

Agnes Savill, *Alexander the Great and His Time*. London: Rockliff Publishers, 1955. Helpful details about the relationships of Alexander with his army.

John Snyder, *Alexander the Great*. New York: Twayne Publishers, 1966. Difficult reading, but interesting notes and quotations.

C.L. Sulzberger, *Fathers and Children: How Famous Leaders Were Influenced by Their Fathers*. New York: Arbor House, 1987. Fascinating account of the relationship between Philip and Alexander.

Additional Works Consulted

Jacob Abbott, *History of Alexander the Great.* New York: Harper and Brothers, 1876. Interesting, very readable telling of the story of Alexander from a nineteenth century point of view.

Arrian, *History of Alexander and Indica.* Translated by P.A. Brunt. Cambridge, MA: Harvard University Press, 1976. Arrian, an early Greek historian, is a valuable source of ancient history.

Maureen Ash, *Alexander the Great.* Chicago: Children's Press, 1991. Very easy reading, well-illustrated.

A.B. Bosworth, *Conquest and Empire: The Reign of Alexander the Great.* Cambridge, England: Cambridge University Press, 1988. Excellent maps, difficult reading.

Trevor Nevitt Dupuy, *The Military Life of Alexander the Great of Macedon, vol. IX.* Translated by Russel M. Geer. Cambridge, MA: Harvard University Press, 1962. *Diodorus of Sicily, vol. VIII.* Translated by Bradford Welles. Cambridge, MA: Harvard University Press, 1963. Both volumes give interesting details of Alexander's life, written by one of the best early historians.

Robin Lane Fox, *The Search for Alexander.* Boston: Little, Brown and Company, 1980. Readable account of Alexander's campaigns, with excellent color photographs of terrain of his empire.

Greece and Rome: Builders of Our World. Edited by Merle Severy. New York: National Geographic Society, 1968. Very readable, good maps, excellent photographs of Alexander's empire.

Peter Green, *Alexander the Great.* New York: Praeger Publishers, 1970.

Finely Hooper, *Greek Realities: Life and Thought in Ancient Greece.* New York: Charles Scribner's Sons, 1967. Excellent bibliography, though the text is difficult reading.

John Keegan, *The Mask of Command.* New York: Viking, 1987. An interesting look at the characteristics that made Alexander a hero.

Stephen Krensky, *Conqueror and Hero.* Boston: Little, Brown and Company, 1981.

Frank Lipsius, *Alexander the Great.* New York: Saturday Review Press, 1974.

Charles Mercer, *Alexander the Great.* New York: American Heritage Publishing, 1962. Easy reading, good illustrations.

Plutarch, *The Age of Alexander.* Translated by Ian Scott-Kilvert. Middlesex, England: Penguin, 1973. One of the most valuable sources of ancient biographies, largely because of Plutarch's style—very readable, with attention to detail.

Mary Renault, *The Nature of Alexander.* New York: Pantheon, 1975. Good presentation of facts, excellent index.

W.W. Tarn, *Alexander the Great.* Boston: Beacon Press, 1956. A thoroughly researched biography with excellent notes.

Index

36-37, 41-44
Thebes destroyed, 41-44
wars with Persia, 31, 35
see also League of Corinth
Greeks
  alliance with Alexander, 43-44, 55
  as slaves, 85-86
  geography of the world, 98
  mercenary soldiers, 52, 53, 54
  Philip's treatment of, 30-31
  Philip's war with, 28-30
  religion and, 37-38, 51, 77, 79
  surrender to Alexander, 56
Green, Peter
  on Alexander's motivation, 114
  on King Darius, 41
  on Philip's murder, 32-33
  on young Alexander, 20-21

Hammond, Nicholas, on Macedon, 15
Hellespont, Alexander crosses, 50-51
Hephestion
  death of, 110-111
  in India, 98
  in Troy, 52
  loyal to Alexander, 66, 90
  marries Persian woman, 108
Hercules, 15, 19, 20
Hindu Kush, 92
Hitler, Adolf, 114
Homer, 23-24, 51, 67
hoplites, 17, 26-27, 72
Hydaspes River, battle of, 99-102

Iliad, 23-24, 51, 67
India
  Alexander explores, 105-108
  Alexander invades, 97-105
Issus, battle of, 64-65

Keegan, John

on Alexander in battle, 42
on Alexander's accession to Macedonian throne, 35
on Alexander's invasion of Persia, 35
on marriage of Philip and Olympias, 19
Krensky, Stephen, on Alexander and Diogenes, 30

League of Corinth
  Alexander takes over, 37, 44
  collapse of, 36
  Philip forms, 31, 32
  supplies ships for Alexander, 57
Leonidas
  gifts from Alexander to, 75
  tutors Alexander, 22
Lipsius, Frank, on siege machines, 59
Louis XIV of France, 114

Macedon
  Alexander rules after Philip's death, 34-36
  Alexander's birthplace, 13
  Alexander's burial and, 10, 11
  Antigonus succeeds Alexander as ruler of, 113
  bankruptcy and, 49
  people of, 15
Marduk (Babylonian god), 84
Memnon, 52
Mercer, Charles, 37
Michelangelo, 115
Midas, King, 60

Napoleon, 114
Nebuchadnezzar, king of Babylonia, 68

Odyssey, 51
Olympias of Macedon (mother of Alexander)
  advice to Alexander, 88
  Alexander sends plunders

to, 54, 67, 75
Alexander's son and, 112
influence on Alexander, 17-18, 19-20, 22, 31
marriage of, 17-18, 22
murders Cleopatra's son, 35-36
plots against Philip, 31-32
  Philip's murder and, 33
religion of, 17-18
unhappy marriage of, 19-20, 31
Olympic Games, 18
Oracle at Delphi, 37, 77, 78
Oracle of Ammon, 77-79
Oxyartes, 96

Parmenio, General
  advice to Alexander, 53, 57, 61, 69-70, 86-87
  death of, 92, 94
  marches into Asia Minor, 32
  supports Alexander for king, 35
Patroclus, 52
Pausanias, murders Philip, 33, 36
Persepolis, plunder of, 85-87
Persia
  Alexander invades
    crosses Hellespont, 50
    Egyptians welcome him, 75
    Gaugamela battle, 81-83
    Granicus River battle, 52-55
    liberates Greeks, 53-55, 56-58, 62
    plans for, 45, 49
    problems at Tyre, 69-71
    victory at, 72-73
    takes Miletus, 57
    takes seacoast, 58
    victory at Gaza, 73-74
    victory at Issus, 64-65, 67
  empire of
    decline of, 47-48
    extent of, 45, 46

Credits

Cover photo by Stock Montage/Historical Pictures

Archiv fur Kunst und Geschichte, Berlin, 9, 90, 112, 115

The Bettmann Archive, 28, 30, 34, 44 (both), 61, 65, 77, 94, 103, 105, 110, 114

Library of Congress, 23 (bottom), 51

North Wind Picture Archives, 12, 14 (both), 15, 18, 38, 41, 47, 52, 57, 59, 70, 71, 74 (bottom), 75, 76, 79 (bottom), 80, 93, 99, 109

Stock Montage/Historical Pictures, 10, 16, 20, 21, 23 (top), 25, 26, 27, 36, 37, 39, 46, 48, 50, 54, 60, 64, 66, 69, 74 (top), 79 (top), 82, 83, 84, 86, 89, 97, 101 (both), 102, 111, 113

Grateful acknowledgment is made to the following publishers for granting permission to quote extensively from copyrighted works:

The Age of Alexander by Plutarch, translated by Ian Scott-Kilvert. Penguin Classics. London: Penguin Books, 1973, pages 253-329. Translation copyright © Ian Scott-Kilvert, 1973. Reproduced by permission of Penguin Books Ltd.

Reprinted by permission of the publishers and Loeb Classical Library from Arrian: *Anabasis Alexandri*, Vols. 1-2, translated by P.A. Brunt, Cambridge, Mass.: Harvard University Press, 1976. Copyright © by the President and Fellows of Harvard College, 1976.

About the Author

Gail B. Stewart received her undergraduate degree from Gustavus Adolphus College in St. Peter, Minnesota. She did her graduate work in English, linguistics, and curriculum study at the College of St. Thomas and the University of Minnesota. Stewart taught English and reading for more than ten years.

She has written over forty-eight books for young people, including a six-part series called *Living Spaces*. She has written several books for Lucent Books including *Drug Trafficking* and *Acid Rain*.

Stewart and her husband live in Minneapolis with their three sons, two dogs, and a cat. She enjoys reading (especially children's books) and playing tennis.